theWitof
CRICKET

the Wit of CRICKET

IAN BRAYSHAW

ANDRE DEUTSCH

First published 1981 by
The Currawong Press Pty Ltd,
in Australia

This edition published 1982 by
André Deutsch Limited
105 Great Russell Street London WCI

Copyright © 1981 by Ian Brayshaw

Produced by Graphic Consultants
International Pte. Ltd., Singapore

ISBN 233 97476 8

FOREWORD by Dennis Lillee

Long years in the game of cricket have taught me a few things. One of them is that where this peculiar form of lifestyle is concerned, nothing surprises. Having said that, I'm in no way surprised that my old teammate and friend Ian Brayshaw has presented another collection of cricket anecdotes. And after a quick read of them, I would suggest that this selection is even more far-reaching and rib-tickling than his first two books on the subject. That's a real indication that as long as cricket is played — at any level, anywhere — there will be odd and humorous happenings. Why not share them around?

When you begin playing first-class cricket you're likely to be the butt of the jokes and the cause of the humour. As time wears on there are plenty of opportunities to get some of your own back — with interest! Certainly when I began playing for Western Australia, back in 1969, the older and more experienced players in the side had no trouble taking a rise out of me. It was all so new. And I was so young and wet behind the ears that I copped my share of jokes on me.

I played my first game in Brisbane, where it rained so much that one afternoon when we left the Gabba at five o'clock, the ground was literally under water. An enterprising newspaper photographer had put his camera down low to the water and pictured a beer can half submerged in the water, indicating that there was an inch or two lying on the outer at that stage. The picture appeared on the front page of the local paper the next morning. My mischievous teammates convinced me that the (beer) can was a 44-gallon drum ... imagine my surprise when we arrived at the ground an hour later and no water!

I was caught time after time that year and even once or twice the following summer when I started playing Test cricket. But I soon realised that the best method of defence was attack. I've been able to get one or two back since those early days. Like the time WA won a very tight game in Adelaide (our first win there for years) and the boys got stuck into some celebratory drinks in the dressingroom. I liked rum and coke in those days, so the manager relented and bought a bottle just for me. One of the youngsters in the side reckoned that rum and coke was his sort of drink, too, so I agreed to share it. We had one with coke, then, acting as though carried away with the euphoria of the win, I suggested we drink straight from the bottle. Trouble for the young chap was that I'd perfected a technique of appearing to be downing heaps though not actually swallowing a drop. Very soon the poor fellow was flat on his back. I was stone cold sober. Terrible, isn't it!

But that's the way with cricket. There are so many long periods of being together as a team during travel, in the dressingroom, out on the field and in between times, that the humour just goes on and on. Hooray for yet another collection of excellent stories — it must be an after-dinner speaker's dream!

INTRODUCTION

Watch a Test match at the Melbourne Cricket Ground and you'll soon find out who are the favourites with the down-to-earth cricket fans who turn up in their droves to dress up the outer section of the ground. The inhabitants of Bay 13, Southern Stand, just about do handstands (if and when capable — a lot depends on the time of day!) whenever Max Walker or Jim Higgs, in particular, come anywhere near the play. And, of course, Dennis Lillee is their absolute joy. Why? Because these are the characters of the game.

Walker because of his strange lanky-legged, tangle-footed bowling action, a wide toothy grin under that perennial floppy white hat, and a dry-as-chips sense of humour. Jim Higgs could almost be described the anti-hero of the MCG outer — they love him more for what he isn't than what he is. They're prouder of their boy when he manages to stop one in the field, or simply lay willow on leather, than they are when he rips through a side with his well-flighted leggies. When Jim stuck around to help Doug Walters make a century in the third Test against New Zealand last season, the screams from the outer as they left the field were more for Jim's courageous six not out that for Douggie's 107! A press cartoon the following day summed it up. It showed the two helmeted men walking off with Jim saying to Doug, 'Next time you can stick around long enough for me to make my "ton"!'

And why do they love Lillee? Sure they love to see him make the opposition batsmen jump during a tight Test match situation. Sure they like to cheer his marvellous performances on the ground which seems to be a home away from home for the champion paceman. But above all they adore the expression in Lillee's bowling — from the awesome run-up, shirt unbuttoned exposing flashing gold medallions on a thick mat of hairy chest; the Lillee shuffle as one goes by the outside edge; the Lillee glare as he thinks there may be a weakness appearing; and those demanding appeals. More than that, though, Lillee is a man's man, afraid of nobody and he is prepared to ham it up, to break the monotony that sometimes dulls good cricket. Above all, Lillee is a dinki-di Aussie.

It's men like these three contemporary players — and, going back, Freddie Trueman, Keith Miller and Colin Milburn — who make cricket the appealing game that it is, who give people something to look forward to and something to talk about during and after. Otherwise, it could and probably would be an awfully ordinary game. I mean, you've got to have a sense of humour to be prepared to sit through five days of a Test match and go away happy with neither side a winner. Yes, there's a peculiar mentality among we cricket-lovers and I hope this collection of memorabilia will stay with you for years. Let's face it, we've got to have something to amuse us when rain stops play ...

THE WIT OF CRICKET

When Dennis Lillee was on his record-breaking trail during the 1980-81 Australian season, many spared a thought for one of the men whose milestone Lillee went streaking past during the Third Test against India at the Melbourne Cricket Ground. That was the great West Australian speedster Graham McKenzie, whose tally of 246 Test victims had stood for a decade — just two short of spinner Richie Benaud's all-time Australian record.

Sympathy for McKenzie stemmed from when at the peak of his career the Australian selectors chose to leave him out of the Test team for two matches — simply because he was bowling too well for the good of the series! McKenzie's scorching speed had so demoralised the Indian batsmen during the first two Tests of the 1967-68 tour of Australia that the 'three wise men' rested him from the final two and instead tried some aspirants for the forthcoming tour of England. This denied McKenzie the opportunity to take maybe a dozen more wickets which would have meant finishing his career ten or so wickets ahead of Benaud's record. McKenzie took it all in his stride. He was, after all, known throughout cricket spheres as the 'gentle giant' of fast bowling. And 'giant' is no understatement. McKenzie's great frame earned him the nickname 'Garth' (after a comic-strip hero) and his superb physique never went unnoticed.

Garth was a callow 19-year-old when he made his first tour of England in 1961 and scorer for that team was Jack Cameron, who has been for many years the Melbourne scorer for the Australian Broadcasting Commission. Jack tells a story about the team's game against Gloucestershire at Bristol. After play one day he was talking to captain Richie Benaud outside the door of the Australian dressingroom when a middle-aged woman approached them. She was selling the Gloucestershire County Cricket Club's booklet and in her naivety thought a trip to the Australian rooms might swell the turnover for the day.

'I'm sorry madam, but you can't go in there,' Benaud told her as she tried to walk past him and enter the room where the Australian players were in various stages of undress. The ardent booklet-seller was persistent.

'I'm sorry,' Benaud repeated, 'but you just can't go in there.' But the woman brushed past Benaud and entered the room — to be confronted by the full-frontal nude frame of McKenzie (who was towelling his hair and quite oblivious to the female intruder).

'I told you that you shouldn't go in,' said Benaud, whereupon the woman dismissed the sight with a haughty:

'Oh *that's* nothing.' Benaud was momentarily taken aback, but pointing at the naked Garth, replied with feigned disbelief:

'Madam, if you think *that's* nothing, you must have been thoroughly spoilt all your life.'

Learie Constantine, who was awarded a peerage for his contribution to cricket and politics, was known throughout the cricket world as a fearsome fast bowler and a dashing batsman for the West Indies. Connie had a style all of his own when flailing the blade. He was noted for one stroke in particular, in which he would take a stride forward, drop down on one knee, and with a tremendous flick of his mighty wrists, thrash and ball through the area between point and cover. It was truly a square drive with a difference. In one of the dressingrooms at the Sydney Cricket Ground hangs a photograph of Connie executing this very stroke. A handwritten caption beneath it tells the story:

'Half drive, half cut ... wholly Constantine.'

In the old days of club cricket in Melbourne there were few greater characters than Les Keating, who for quite some time was captain of the Richmond Cricket Club's first team. Ernie McCormick, a tall, lean and taciturn fast bowler who played 12 Tests for Australia in the 1930s, tells a story about his young days at the Richmond club under the captaincy of Keating. He recalls a game at the Punt Road Ground when he was last man in with just ten runs required for victory. Ernie tells it this way:

'I admit I wasn't much of a bat in those days. My teammates were well aware of this, too, so before I went in I got plenty of advice from them about keeping my head down, playing straight and leaving the run-scoring to the bloke at the other end. As it turned out, Les Keating was the fellow at the other end when I went in. He buttonholed me on the way out and told me to keep my head down, to play straight and leave the scoring to him. Well and truly fortified by all of this advice, I took guard and faced up. The first ball was well up and without thinking I took a wild swipe at it and away the thing went over square leg, out on to Punt Road. Les and I met in the middle of the wicket and the old fellow put his arm on my shoulder and said, "That's the way son, head down and play straight ... the shots can come later".'

How's this for an example of a batsman — and his team — getting on with the job! It occurred when Australia sent a team to New Zealand during the summer of 1913-14. The game in question was against Canterbury. The batsman was the legendary Victor Trumper. He scored a rather brisk 293 himself while his team ended up all out for 653, the innings taking just 385 minutes. A contemporary report shows that the Aussies skipped from the 550 mark to their all-out score of 653 in a mere 21 minutes. And no wonder, when you have a look at Trumper's innings in segments of 50: 26 minutes, for the first, 47 for the second, 19 the third, 39 the fourth and 21 the fifth. That's 250 runs off his own bat in 152 minutes. In all he was at the crease for 180 minutes for his 293!

Capturing 'all-ten' wicket in an innings has been achieved only once in the history of New Zealand first-class cricket. Way back in the 1889-90 season a gentleman called A.E. Moss claimed 10-28 for Canterbury against Wellington ... in his debut, if you don't mind! That record has stood all these years, but it was given a real shake in the 1928-29 season when, but for a cruel misfortune, the Canterbury player D.J. McBeath would have become No. 2.

Playing against Auckland at Christchurch, McBeath bowled unchanged through the innings to claim the first nine wickets to fall. Sensing an historical performance, McBeath put everything into his first delivery to the No. 11 batsman

Coates, who responded by spooning a catch to mid-on, where McEwin dropped a sitter. As if to add salt to the wound, McEwin in the very next over proceeded to take Coates's wicket — and poor McBeath finished with 9–56. You don't have to be dead to be stiff!

There have been countless minor and major changes to the laws of cricket as the game has been refined over the years. One area which, for some reason, hasn't been as stable as it might is the method of deciding when a new ball should become available. The lawmakers have been undecided whether this arbitrary decision should be based on the number of runs scored or the number of balls bowled. These days it relates to the latter — after 85 six-ball overs have been bowled in Test matches, and after 100 overs have been bowled in Sheffield Shield games in Australia. But in a day gone by, the new ball could be taken after 200 runs had been scored. So, picture the scene in Bombay when an Australian team called there on its way to England in the 1930s...

The tourists were being introduced rather ceremoniously to a very wealthy and influential Maharajah. As the players stood in two neat lines awaiting the great moment of introduction, they were addressed by the team manager:

'I would like very much to introduce you to the Maharajah of So-and-so... not only is he the richest man in the world, but he also has 199 wives.'

From the depths of the back row came the quip:

'One more and he'd need a new ball!'

When he was at his peak, fiery Freddie Trueman was enough to frighten the living daylights out of the stoutest Test batsmen of the day. The Yorkshire and England speedster could make them all squirm... Spare a thought for that worried little Indian batsman who came out to face up to Trueman's fury. After having taken his guard, he was carefully marking it on the crease when the sympathetic umpire helpfully asked if the sightscreen position was suitable.

'I b-beg your p-pardon,' stammered the shaking Indian.

'Do you want the sightscreen moved?' repeated the umpire.

Coming to his senses a little, the batsman said meekly:

'Yes, it would help a little if it could be moved... preferably to a position somewhere between me and (pointing to Trueman at the top of his mark some fifty metres away) that snorting brute back there!'

Apart from being one of the truly great all-rounders cricket has ever seen, Keith Miller gained a name as a debonair, devil-may-care character of the game. His reputation was for performing when his team was in a tight corner, but with a tendency to take matters rather lightly on occasions when they were right on top. Perhaps there was no greater example of that situation than the Essex game on the 1948 tour of England, when Australia made a record 721 runs on the first day. The top part of the Australian scoresheet read: 'Barnes 79, Brown 153, Bradman 187, Miller 0, Hamence 46, Loxton 120, Saggers 104 not out'.

But the record books show that more often than not Miller produced when he was needed. While on tour, particularly in England, he tended to live the high life whenever the opportunity arose, a habit that caused his captains a few headaches. Imagine a rather agitated Australian team waiting to leave their hotel to travel together to the ground for a match in England, when into the foyer dashes Miller, hair flying in typical fashion — resplendant in his evening attire!

Always professional, Geoff Boycott checks his gear during a break.

For sheer beauty of batting technique you couldn't look past the great England opener, Geoff Boycott. Throughout his long, run-packed career, Boycott has demonstrated the value of precision and correctness in strokeplay, promoting the principle that if you don't hit the ball in the air you can't be caught. But the dour Yorkshireman has won few friends outside his County — and even they turned on him and summarily removed him from the Yorkshire captaincy (a post he had sought and covetted).

The reasons for this lack of popularity were twofold. Firstly, folk grew weary of admiring the beauty of a batting technique that had, in eliminating risks, virtually closed most avenues of run-scoring. His innings became drawn-out wars of attrition with his opponents, and spectators. Indeed, he once suffered the indignity of being dropped from the England team after making a Test double century. He had been just too slow! Secondly, for one reason or another Boycott is by nature a loner, a man who shuns relationships with teammates and, above all, the press and the fans. People can endure dour play, perhaps, if the man behind it is a lovable character. Boycott does not qualify. A pointer to his introverted nature is his recent tour agreements with the MCC: he had to have a room to himself, a privilege usually reserved for the captain.

Back to Boycott the batsman. If he was to have had a bete noire during his long Test career it might have been the mystery spinner from New South Wales, John Gleeson. The droll country boy from Tamworth had Boycott and his teammates tied in knots during the 1970–71 tour of Australia. They just couldn't pick which way the ball was going to spin off Gleeson's middle finger. Boycott was no exception, so the dyed-in-the-wool professional spirit went to work. He studied the Tamworth Twister's action for hours until finally he cracked it. If it looked as though Gleeson was bowling an off-break it would in fact be a leggie, and vice versa.

Boycott was out there one day, putting his discovery to the test, when he was approached by his partner at the time, breezy Basil d'Oliveira, who announced that he had just worked out how to pick Gleeson's spin. This came as a blow to Boycott, who liked to be one jump ahead of everybody, even his teammates in a Test match.

'Have you then,' he said, a frown furrowing his brow, 'shall we not tell the others?'

A balmy afternoon during a Test match at the Melbourne Cricket Ground was rudely interrupted by a between-overs announcement through the public address system.

'Would Mr J. Smith of Hawthorn please go home,' the voice announced, 'your wife is having her baby and must be taken to hospital.'

Laughter flowed around the ground as the spectators pictured a harrassed father-to-be hurrying off home to his wife. Not so, however, because about half an hour the voice again boomed across the ground, this time with some urgency:

'Repeating our earlier message to Mr J. Smith of Hawthorn ... would he please go home immediately, because his wife is in labour and must be taken to hospital straight away.'

Much more mirth from the crowd, this time picturing a man reluctant to leave the cricket — but surely by now bidding farewell to his mates to dash to his vehicle and tear off home. How wrong were 20,000 spectators! Much to their delight, the now pleading message was repeated with grim urgency some 20 minutes later. After a further 30 minutes passed there was a bland announcement:

'Would Mr J. Smith of Hawthorn please go to the Mercy Hospital, where his wife has now given birth to a baby son!'

There's a terrible finality about the broadcast word. Once it has taken off on the air waves, there's no retrieving. You're stuck with it forever ... and every man who has ever tried his hand at off-the-cuff commentary has, at some time or another, opened his mouth wide and plunged his foot right in. Even the legendary Alan McGilvray of the ABC radio commentary team occasionally doesn't get things quite how he might have meant them to be. Like the time in the heart of the 1980-81 season when he summed up a batting failure by Kim Hughes this way: 'Well, it has been a weekend of delight and disappointment for Kim Hughes — his wife presented him with twins yesterday ... and a "duck" today!'

The legendary W.C. Grace was without doubt the peerless batsman of his time and the story has it that modesty was not his problem. He gave ample evidence of this when playing a game in a country town during a tour to Australia. He faced the first delivery of the game from a rough bushie. To the surprised delight of the bowler and his teammates the champion was clean bowled. But their joy was shortlived. 'I never could play the trial ball,' said W.G., as he replaced the bails and took up his stance again. The bowler, quite naturally, wasn't taking this lying down and protested strongly, whereupon the bearded Englishman replied, 'Look here, these people have paid to come and see me bat, not you bowl ... now let's get on with it'.

George Headley was one of the great early West Indian batsmen. He played just 22 Tests, yet scored ten centuries with a top score 270 and averaged just over 60. So it was no wonder that people compared him with the Australian run-machine of the time, Don Bradman. In his latter years Headley was asked how he had felt about being called the 'Black Bradman'. His eyes twinkled as he replied, 'I've wondered for years if Sir Donald knew that in the West Indies he was known as the "White Headley".'

We read these days of fire-breathing fast bowlers whose main aim is to rip a few short ones into a new batsman to assert their authority from the start. With most teams boasting three or four fast bowlers, that can be a harrowing experience in which only the truly stern of spirit prevail. But picture the situation in reverse when Charlie Macartney was in his prime as a batsman for Australia. It is said of this aggressive striker of the ball that he liked to get on top of the bowling immediately and did so in the best way he knew: By thumping a couple straight back at the bowler as hard as he could to take a bit of the sting out of him.

Fine English slow bowler Hedley Verity had such control of line and length that he very rarely came in for rough treatment. But there's always that one occasion. It happened when a big-hitter from South Africa, H.G. Cameron, slammed two sixes and three fours off the usually unruffled Verity. At the end of the over one of Verity's teammates said 'Well you've got him in two minds, Hedley.' Verity's brow furrowed. 'In two minds, what do you mean?' he said. 'He doesn't know whether to hit you for four or six!'

When the Pakistan team was in Australia in the 1976-77 season, opening batsman Majid Khan started the tour in Perth wearing a rather grubby off-white washer hat. Dennis Lillee was struck by the stark contrast between this hat and

the rest of Majid's immaculately-clean gear, not to mention his fastidiously correct manner. During the First Test in Adelaide, Lillee noticed that Majid was still wearing the (by now even-dirtier) hat. He felt compelled to ask the Pakistani about it and was told with a flashing smile:

'Oh, you might call it superstition. But since I started wearing it my luck has been good, I daren't wash it in case my luck changes.'

End of subject? No. Lillee eyed the hat curiously for a few seconds, which prompted a response. 'If you can knock it off, you can have it,' said Majid. Lillee had completely forgotten the promise when he thundered in to let Majid have a short one during the third and final Test at Sydney. The ball really took off and struck the Pakistani a grazing blow on the head, knocking him to the ground and sending the dirty old washer hat flying. The Australian fieldman hurried to Majid's assistance, but quick as a flash he bounced to his feet, picked up the hat and with a toothy grin walked up to his adversary and offered him the hat.

'You were good enough to knock it off — it's yours,' he said.

The West Australian team had a shocking fit of the fumbles in their Sheffield Shield game against Queensland in Brisbane at the start of the 1980–81 season. On the first day they dropped Queensland's star batsman Greg Chappell five times before he had reached a century and seven times in all before he was finally dismissed. To make matters worse, they had dropped several other catches on that day. Early on the following day a strong wind sprang up, complicating matters for the WA bowler who had to push up into it. Commentator Dennis Cometti was just going through the motions of explaining this to his listeners when an incident out in the middle caught his eye.

'That's really bad luck for WA,' he said, closing the one subject '...but now some good news for the side — a gust of wind has just blown Rob Langer's hat off in the slips and Kim Hughes has caught it!'

Cricket commentators can get themselves into some pretty precarious positions — especially at grounds not designed for cricket. And that's just what happened when India played the West Australian Country XI at the rural town of Harvey during their 1967–68 tour of Australia. The ground at Harvey was laid out for Australian Rules football and trotting. So the temporary broadcast position for the ABC's commentator, George Grljusich, was on the back of truck parked at the boundary edge on the trotting track at one end of the ground. George's technical assistant that day, an English-born cricket fanatic called Eric Hill, was also acting as the scorer for the broadcast. The pair were reasonably happy carrying out their duties from this position when the Indian captain, the Nawab of Pataudi, let fly and lofted the ball straight back over the bowler's head and right on target for the truck top. Grljusich tried to catch the ball but missed and it flew through to hit Hill, who was wearing a pair of shorts, a very painful blow on the inside of his right thigh. Immediately a bright red weal showed up on his leg and the game stopped while the players jogged down to check on his well-being. Somewhat fortified by their presence, Hill reached for his pen, muttered with a forced grin:

'I suppose I'd better mark it down as a six' — and, using the outline of the ball as a circle, marked the remainder of the figure '6' on his leg!

The great Don Bradman at the nets in the 30s.

Some suggest it is a mistake to appoint a bowler to captain a cricket team, because he either bowls himself too little or too much. Legend has it that it was invariably a case of the latter when Johnny Douglas captained England. Bowlers in Douglas's teams were known to mutter to each other when a new batsman came in, 'You go on now and bowl him in, Mr Douglas ... we'll come on later and bowl him out.' One day Douglas had gone on for so long that one of them felt moved to approach him:

'Don't you think it's time we had a change in the attack, Mr Douglas?'

'You could be right,' came the reply, 'I'll have a go at the other end.'

Sir Donald Bradman spent so much of his playing days pouring salt into the wounds of English cricket teams that he wasn't about to be associated too closely with them at a reception in Adelaide during the 1970-71 tour. He arrived at the reception just after the MCC players, who had signed the visitors book, putting after their names 'MCC team'. When Sir Donald added his name to the book, he wrote after it, 'Not MCC team!'

At the start of the 1974-75 season, the Australian cricket team was set to launch into an era in which it would dominate the international scene. Jeff Thomson was about to join Dennis Lillee to give the side its most potent attacking force since Lindwall and Miller in the 1950s and there was a look of depth to the batting. Going up to Brisbane for the First Test against England, there was only one batsman in the Australian line-up whose form was worrying — Doug Walters. The New South Wales dasher hadn't had the best of series against England in 1970-71 (in Australia) and 1972 (in

England) and he was coming into this game with an average for the season that was down in the 'teens.

Walters himself must have been a bit concerned. Well, just a tiny bit, because he shocked his teammates by arriving at the nets on the morning of the first day of the Test. It was such a rare sight, Walters *practising,* that he was immediately the centre of attention. He had brought along a bat and ball and he proceeded to 'practise'. First he tossed the ball in the air with the obvious intention of hitting it into the side of the nets, just to 'feel' the ball on the bat. But the ball wasn't there — it landed on his shoulder. Now *everybody* was watching! The second throw produced the desired result and Doug hit it right in the middle. 'I'm seeing them much better now,' he declared, and without even stopping to pick up the ball, he headed back to the dressingroom.

Veteran ABC commentators Alan McGilvray and Lindsay Hassett were far from impressed by the decision to move the broadcast box at the Adelaide Oval for the 1980–81 season. They had rather enjoyed their previous position, an unimpeded view on a scaffolding above the sightscreen and in the shelter of the giant moreton bay fig trees at the northern end of the ground. The new position was right at the back of the Creswell Stand at the southern (or River Torrens) end. The same spot from which they'd covered Tests for the ABC back in the late 1950s. Up in the new elevated position for the Second Test against the Indians in 1980–81, they found their view of the ground impeded by a huge pylon and a television camera platform. What was worse, their tiny broadcast box was placed right up under the tin roof of the stand. In the blistering heat that prevailed throughout the Test, going inside for a stint was like stepping into a sauna fully clothed.

Hassett took a thermometer in on one of the days and got a reading of 42C! As if that wasn't enough to daunt them, the long, long straight drives at the Adelaide Oval meant that the position was so far from the wicket that binoculars became an almost mandatory appendage. The box was so cramped that any change of commentator involved a degree of cooperation up there, so McGilvray suggested that his mate move back to allow him to take his seat at the mike.

'Move back,' exclaimed Hassett. 'If I took six steps backwards I'd fall into the Torrens!'

Former England fast bowler Freddie Trueman is one of the grand characters of the game. During his incomparable playing days for Yorkshire and his country, Trueman provided a marvellous blend of the very serious nature of the game at its highest competitive levels and occasional light relief. He was indeed quite fierce about wicket-taking in Tests. He held the world record for the number of dismissals for at time, with 307 victims (topped later by West Indies spinner Lance Gibbs, whose mark of 309 still stands). Freddie was a truly fearsome sight as he stormed in to let the quickies fly — and he followed through with a savage and sometimes withering glare for the batsman. He was, however, no great shakes as a batsman. His lighter side surfaced when the boot was on the other foot and he found himself facing a West Indian speedster in a Test in England a few years back. After watching a couple whistle past his nose to the wicketkeeper, fiery Freddie responded by sinking to his knees on the pitch, clasping his gloved hands together and raising his eyes to the heavens in prayer. It brought the house down.

Since his playing days ended Freddie has been sharing his dry wit with listeners to the BBC coverage of Test cricket in England. And a good example of how a Northern Englishman can turn a rather mundane situation into a hoot came during one of the one-day internationals at the start of the

1981 Australian tour of England. Australian fast bowler Geoff Lawson was operating and the ball-by-ball commentator at the time had dwelt ad nauseum on the considerable length of Lawson's legs. Finally he asked Trueman if he agreed. The dour Freddie replied: 'Aye, and perhaps that's why the lad's so tall!'

Not many bowlers had much joy when Sir Donald Bradman went about the business of making runs. His career record of scoring a century once in every three first-class innings he played is ample proof of that. As well as being absolute master with the bat on the field, the Don was very rarely shaded when it came to a battle of wits off the field. Like the time when the Australians were on tour and a few of the lads were filling in the hours when rain had stopped play with a game of poker. The players were shocked when the Don came over and asked to join the school, but eagerly offered him a chair. Immediately a couple of them began slipping the inexperienced newcomer a losing card here and there and it wasn't long before the Don was losing a considerable amount of money. All of a sudden the master batsman realised what was happening. Without batting an eyelid he rose, pocketed all the money on the table and left with a smiling riposte:
    'If you can't play it fair, we don't play at all.'

Terry Jenner was a very good leg-spinner for South Australia during the 1960s and 1970s, but he was nothing if not renowned for having his fair share to say both on and off the field. And at times he wasn't too fussy in his choice of words. Well aware this, his teammates and his West Australian opponents thought it almost appropriate when, as he ran in to bowl during a game at the Adelaide Oval, a bird flying directly overhead bombed its droppings fair and square on Jenner's mouth. The players, who were rolling on the ground in their mirth as 'T.J.' cleaned up, almost missed a moment of rare humility from their leggie.

'Quite appropriate, I suppose,' he said, pointing to his mouth, 'there's been quite a bit of the same coming out over the years.'

The Indian cricket team made a most disappointing start to its three-Test series in Australia in 1980–81. The tourists went down by an innings in the First Test, which began in Sydney just after Christmas. The margin was largely due to a fighting double century by Australian Greg Chappell, but aided by some most irresponsible strokeplay by the Indians. After the game, the Indian captain Sunil Gavaskar was asked for his comments on the ignominious defeat. The little fellow forced a smile and summed it up this way:

'We gave away our wickets like Christmas presents ... trouble is, we Indians don't celebrate Christmas!'

Back in the early 1960s, West Indian express bowler Roy Gilchrist signed on as the professional for Bacup in the Lancashire League competition. 'Gilly' was frighteningly quick for most batsmen in the league and on some grounds his long approach to the wicket began with a push off the sightscreen. The main problem for Bacup was trying to hold catches off his bowling. Derek Whitworth vividly recalls the first time the West Indian stripped for the club, which also happened to be 16-year-old Derek's first appearance for the first team. It was a bitterly cold day on Bacup's ground, high in the Pennines and the captain liberally sprinkled all but a couple of his men in behind-the-wickets catching positions. Derek ended

up in slips and took a hot one in Gilly's first over. Says Derek: 'On reflection that was a big mistake. Gilly came running straight up to me and shouted "you stay in slips" ... I did for the rest of the season and received so many bruises along the way I wished a hundred times I'd dropped that first one.'

Nobody enjoys being taken to task by a traffic patrolman after having been caught for speeding. Sitting and suffering while the policeman dresses you down, takes the relevant details and hands you the ticket is as much fun as a trip to the dentist's chair ... there's nothing you can do but cop it sweet. Fast bowling champion Dennis Lillee found himself in that predicament when he went a few kilometres over the limit on a dual carriageway near his home in the suburbs of Perth. Though it went against his grain, he sat there and quietly took his medicine, so to speak. After the lecture and note-taking, the officer handed over the ticket. Lillee snatched at the starter to get as far from the scene as possible before he blew a gasket, but the policeman stopped him in his tracks.

'Wait a minute, Mr Lillee,' he said.

'Yes?' came the gruff retort.

'Would you mind giving me an autograph for my young block — he's a fan of yours.'

Expletives deleted!

There's absolutely no holding the dyed-in-the-wool cricket-lover. Many an Englishman, Yorkshireman in particular, in recent years has insisted that his son and heir be named Geoffrey (after Boycott) and there are plenty of Australians now in their thirties and forties who were named Donald at the insistence of father whose adulation of Donald Bradman was an inspiration.

These fanatics also have habit of naming their houses, their boats — and even their pet animals — after their cricketing heroes. Like the devoted follower of West Australian teams and players who gave a home to a couple of stray cats and immediately dubbed them 'Lillee' and 'Massie'. And if you thought that was devotion to a cause, what about the cricket freak of a day gone by who called his dog 'Ponny' after the great Victorian and Australian batsman Bill Ponsford. Alas, Ponny passed away, ironically during the bitter Bodyline series of 1932-33. Being an animal lover, the owner soon replaced the lost pet and the new pooch got the name of 'Larwood' ... because it had four short legs and its balls swung both ways!

One of the most remarkable happenings in the long history of international cricket occurred on December 14, 1960, at the Brisbane Cricket Ground when the first Test between Australia and the West Indies ended in a tie — the first and only tie in the annals of Test cricket. An incredible final day's play, with fortunes fluctuating, culminated in a gripping last over by the West Indies fast bowler Wes Hall. The duration of the over was about fifteen minutes: Three wickets fell, five runs were scored and a simple catch dropped. Twenty years almost to the day after that memorable occasion, lovable Wes Hall was the guest speaker at the New Zealand Sports Star of the Year presentations. The jovial big fellow chose to tell of the dying throes of a great game in which, as he said afterwards, all 24 participants (the umpires included) could have qualified to win the 1960 Sports Star of the Year award. Those who saw the game or read accurate reports of it will realise that in the following speech, Wes Hall used a little poetic licence:

You may well recall that as we went in to the last day Australia were left 233 runs to win, just before lunch. As we walked out Sir Frank Worrell, that great man, said:

"Winfield," he always called me Winfield (Hall's middle name)," today is the day ... today is the day that you will show them what you can do."

Always ready to accept a challenge, I said, "Skipper, if you feel so, just keep your eyes on me and you'll see".

Australia slumped dramatically to 57 for five. I just happened to be lucky enough to collect four of them. One more wicket fell at 92, then, miraculously, Richie Benaud and Alan Davidson seemed to stem the tide. They batted beautifully and when Davidson departed, Australia had a mere eight to get.

At a quarter to six that day, Frank Worrell called me over and he said:

"Winfield, I said today is the day."

"Keep your eyes on me!," I replied.

Fifteen minutes to go and as far as I was concerned it had to be one over to go. If it was more than one over it meant we were beaten, so one over it would be. The first ball I bowled to Wally Grout hit him in the groin. He wasn't interested in a run, no doubt, but Benaud was captain and he called. So Grout hobbled through like a broken-down trotter and collected one run. The second ball Benaud played neatly backward of square and tried to take a run. The ball was thrown to me only about an inch from the wicket. "Brilliant" Hall chose to throw the ball rather than just take off the bails, so Benaud survived.

And the third ball ... well, that brought comment from the captain.

"I'm watchin' you!" he said, "Now look here, Winfield, Grout will be hooking you, so make sure he hooks a yorker."

As I ran up I decided that all I would do was to pitch the ball up. I managed it, and Grout's bat was all up here and then suddenly he had to get down there and the ball somehow took the edge and went straight up to the heavens. There were 13 people out there who could take that catch. The wicketkeeper had gloves on, the slips were there, backward short leg (the ball went rather short of mid-wicket) ... As I had bowled the ball and ended up two yards from the batsman, I thought to myself, "Well let's have a go at this" and I took off. Not seeing Rohan Kanhai in my path I completely knocked him over as he just waited to take the ball. The ball hit my hands and richocheted another 20 yards, so I had to go for that too. After all the confusion I just said, "The good Lord has gone and left us". Kanhai said things that were not printable then — and are not printable now — but I must say they were not complimentary to mother and father.

Well, as I told you the over had to take 15 minutes. The captain called me over and he said:

"Winfield, I'm still watching you! But what ever you do now, do not bowl a bouncer to Richie Benaud.!"

"Okay skipper, you just watch me," I said. I walked back, still very hurt at the shame, the scandal of dropping that catch. My teammates were telling me, "we always knew you couldn't even catch a cold". But as I walked further back, I had other things in mind. I became very purposeful, I felt that if only I could just get this man now, four and a half million people in the West Indies would really come awake ... and since it was half past three in the morning that would have been an achievement. So I turned, looked around, fingered my cross, prayed a little prayer, pulled at my trousers and took off. God was merciful because as I pounded the turf after bowling for fours hours I found that there was a little pep in my step, a little spring in my heels, so I said, "Eh, eh ... let's go, Benaud". I ran up, forgetting all that the captain had said and bowled the fastest bouncer that I've ever bowled in my life. Benaud, seemingly surprised, shaped for the hook but was too late ... alas, it took the glove and there was Jerry Alexander flinging himself in the air, taking the catch and rolling over in great triumph. I swung round, my arms upraised, going towards my captain, hoping he would embrace me... but all I got was a stony silence and a wicked stared.

"He's out skipper, he's out!" I shouted.

"What did I tell you?" he said.

"He's out, he's out!" I said. And then the joke was no more.

"Do you really understand what would have happened had that ball taken the top edge and gone for four runs?" he said.

For the first time in 12 minutes I remembered that Australia needed four runs to win. So there I was again, in deep despair, a batsman out but still no joy. The new batsman came in, Ian Meckiff. He took guard, a monumental rabbit ... surely he would not be able to stand the test. I moved in, but my spirit was broken. How could a man get a wicket and yet be admonished by his captain? And as I walked in, meekly, I bowled just as meekly and Meckiff hit it just as sweetly to the mid-wicket boundary, seemingly. They ran one, they ran two, they ran three ... the ball went right to the boundary, perhaps a yard short and there was Conrad Hunte, not giving up, chasing all the way. He picked up the ball and threw it with remarkable accuracy back to the wicketkeeper, who did not have to move an inch. He took the ball and stumps and there was Grout, sprawled on ground and two yards out of this crease.

So another man was out and the skipper came up to me.

"You've got one ball to go", he said.

"I know."

"And I'm watching you", he said.

"I know."

"And what is more, the umpire is watching you, too".

I didn't understand.

"What are you saying?" I said.

"Well, listen, one ball to go and if you bowl a no-ball you will never be able to land in Barbados again!"

It was then that I saw the predicament I was in. Frank Worrell, as cunning as he was, called me over again as I made my way back.

"I have nothing to tell you ... but the problem is that batsman doesn't know I have nothing to tell you ... so, if I move the man at backward square leg two feet to the right and then two feet to the left he won't know that I have nothing to tell you."

So he did just that — there was Joe Solomon, two feet to the right and then two feet to the left. I made my last lonesome trek back forty yards away from the stumps. I came in, gulping for air and pressing through for the last ball, my feet planted some three yards behind the crease ... just in case we had a benevolent Australian umpire! Lindsay Kline turned the ball backward of square. It looked like an easy run and it was, really. Until Solomon, little Joe Solomon, moved smartly to his left, picked up the ball and, with just one stump to see, threw and hit it bull's eye. The square leg umpire, an Australian, jumped four feet in the air and but gave him out. And Meckiff was heard to say as he returned rather disconsolately to the pavilion, "Fancy losing like that!"

The West Indian cricketers were sure they hadn't lost ... ten men were out weren't they? But we didn't know if we had won, either. So we all went off the ground and the umpires and players all gathered into one dressingroom. Frank Worrell, great captain as he was, came in and just sank in his chair and never moved for another four hours. We drank champagne there and finally dinner was summoned from the Lennons Hotel and we didn't leave there until 10.30 that night. At the end of the series in Melbourne, 80,000 people, young girls, young boys, old girls and old boys, came to

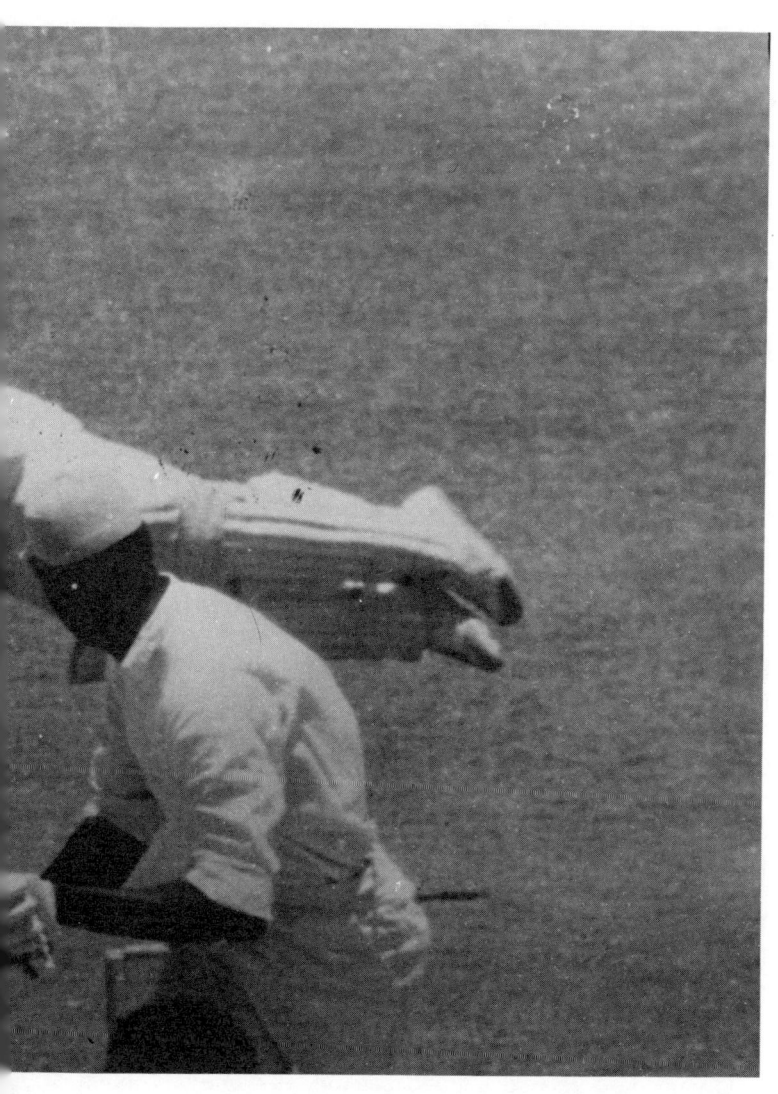

Marsh picks ups Clive Lloyd (Australia v Rest of World, 1971-2)

tell us they thought we were wonderful and that we had done a great service to cricket.

[For the purist: ... *Ball one, Grout is hit in the groin and a stolen single; ball two, Benaud is caught trying to hook a bouncer; ball three, Meckiff plays back to the bowler; ball four, ball down the leg side and a cheeky bye run; ball five, Grout skies the ball and Hall drops the catch, one run taken; ball six, Meckiff swings to leg and Grout is run out attempting a third run; ball seven, Kline pushes to leg and Meckiff is run out when Solomon hits the stumps from side-on.*]

At the end of the England tour of Australia in 1978-79, Robin Bailhache and Dick French, two of the three main umpires used during the six-Test series, received a surprise package in the mail. Each opened his parcel to find a used cricket pad with a note attached, reading, 'From me to you ... guess who!' They were puzzled for a while but after discussing the mystery together they reckoned it could only have come from the England opener, Geoff Boycott. Between them they'd given him out leg-before-wicket four times during the series. And he'd had an awful tour, averaging just 21.92 from twelve Test innings. The two thought nothing more about it, not even when Boycott returned with the England side the following summer. The dour opener did better with the bat this time round and the only leg-before verdict against him in a Test was given when neither Bailhache nor French was standing. However, at the end of the final Test in Melbourne Bailhache couldn't resist the temptation to approach the Yorkshireman.

'Now if you've got anything to give me,' he said, 'give it to me now and don't send it in the post.'

'Oh no, you've had a good season, it's okay,' replied an amused Boycott.

Cricket, more than other sports, inspires droves of enthusiastic statistics buffs. Fact-and-figure data can certainly enhance appreciation of the game, when within reason. But some are prepared to spend countless hours poring over scoresheets in a search for some statistic, however obscure. Indeed, among the players it becomes something of a joke at times, provoking such dressingroom comments as, 'My goodness, that's the first time that two left-handed batsmen have made a partnership of more than fifty in a Sheffield Shield game at the Melbourne Cricket Ground at 2.30 pm on a Monday in January, 1981!' Still the enthusiasts persist, God bless 'em, and produce such gems of international importance as this one from a recent New Zealand publication on the subject: 'When R.J. Hadlee was dismissed for 103 v West Indies at Christchurch, it was the first time a NZ batsman had recorded that score in a Test. This now means that NZ batsmen have made every total from 0 to 105 in Test cricket.' All hail the inveterate stats men!

One of the dark happenings of the 1980–81 Australian summer was the 'underarm incident' during the third World Series Cup final between Australia and New Zealand at the Melbourne Cricket Ground. With just one ball remaining and with the Kiwis needing six runs to tie the match, Greg Chappell instructed his younger brother Trevor to bowl a play-safe underarm delivery. The umpires were informed. They in turn told the incoming batsman, rank tailender Brian McKechnie, who merely blocked the ensuing delivery and threw away his bat in disgust. There began a controversy that brought to an angry boil Australian and international feeling. It wasn't that Greg Chappell had gone outside the laws of cricket ... more that he had acted outside the spirit of a game that had

Greg Chappell on his way to a century in his maiden Test innings, 1970–71

long been recognised as a standard-setter in sportsmanship.

Perhaps the degree of feeling was exacerbated by the fact that earlier in the same day Greg Chappell himself had stood his ground after apparently having been brilliantly caught in the outfield by Martin Snedden off Lance Cairns. The New Zealander had run some 25 metres in the deeps at mid-wicket and dived headlong to apparently snap up the ball millimetres off the grass in what was a memorable effort. Chappel was uncertain as to whether the catch had been made cleanly and declined to walk off, despite the fact that Snedden had held the ball up and that a nearby fieldsman had also signified a clean catch. The Australian captain was within his rights to remain if he had any doubts about the catch and the matter went to the umpires, who gave the batsman the benefit of the doubt that existed. Much heated debate raged between the New Zealanders and the umpires — but the decision stood and Chappell, who was on 58 at the time, continued. He had moved to 90 when he was caught in exactly the same circumstances, this time by Bruce Edgar off the bowling of Snedden. This time Chappell walked on the indication of the fieldsman that the catch had been taken.

But back to that underarm delivery. The hue and cry that followed must have stirred memories of the days of bodyline bowling when feeling also ran high right across the nation. Greg Chappell was the almost unanimous target for a tirade of abuse from critics and the public. There were calls for his sacking or resignation from the captaincy. Even the Prime Ministers of Australia and New Zealand were brought into the matter.

Finally Chappell emerged from hiding to issue a statement deploring his action, explaining that it was the act of a tired man who was fearful that one almighty swipe by McKechnie could have forced his weary team to play another game in the finals series. He'd had enough — so had his players — Chappell reasoned.

The apology defused the issue and by the time Chappell appeared again for Australia two days after the incident the cheers of support outweighted the sporadic boos that were heard. Quite naturally there was more than one humorous sidelight to the ugly affair, thus keeping the matter in proportion with day-to-day life.

The day after the incident the New Zealand team travelled from Melbourne to Sydney for the next encounter in the final round and there, in the foyer of their Sydney hotel on a prominently-displayed board, was a greeting under the heading of 'Quotation of the Day'. It was in fact the final few lines of Sir Henry Newbold's famous cricketing poem about bumping pitches and blinding light and read, 'His captain's hand on his shoulder smote, play up, play up and play the game.' When the team left the hotel a couple of days later to return to New Zealand (beaten 3–1 in the finals) the same notice board bore following farewell message: 'New Zealand one, Australia one, umpires two.'

Before that, though, the press and the public had come out in force to see just what might happen when the two teams met in the fourth final at the Sydney Cricket Ground. As it turned out, Chappell's apology had taken a lot of the sting out of the issue and the New Zealanders, led by their grand captain Geoff Howarth, showed great sportsmanship to illustrate that as far as they were concerned the business was dead and buried. Dennis Lillee couldn't resist the temptation, when having a practice run-up for the first ball of the Kiwis' innings, to go through the motions of an underarm delivery — much to the delight of the huge crowd that had gathered. And the signwriters were out in strength. Perhaps this banner in the Bradman Stand capsulated the feelings of most towards the incident, 'GREGORY — YOUR UNDERARM STINKS'.

There was at least one person who still remembered the matter the next time the Australians played at the MCG — in the Third Test against the Indians the following weekend. A placard above Bay 15 in the Southern Stand drew reference to one of Australia's greatest underarm (lawn) bowlers when it said simply, 'THE JOHN SNELL STAND'. And Rod Marsh, who has always had an eye for a laugh in and around a cricket match, also got into the act. During the Indian Test spinner Jim Higgs let one slip and it bounced three or four times before reaching Shivlal Yadav (who promptly despatched it to the boundary).

'Oh never mind,' said Marsh to the Indian with a grin, 'Jim's just practising his overarm underarm for next season's one-day matches!'

Perhaps the whole matter should rest there.

There are many male chauvinists in the cricket world who believe that in no circumstances should women and cricket be mixed. Imagine the state of mind of the Long Room regulars at Lord's when it was decided to allow women's cricket teams to step on to the turf of their famous ground to play a Test match a few summers back! The hallowed halls were ringing with emptiness in their protest.

Yet a vital development in cricket as we now know it came through a woman who, unable to deliver a ball in the traditional underarm style because of the bulkiness of her bustles, raised many an eyebrow by sending down a roundarm scorcher. From that feminine feat men went on to evolve roundarm and finally the overarm deliveries of today. So one would think that — if only in due deference to that crucial contribution — men would look more kindly on the place of women in cricket. However, the fact most of them don't, is not always man's fault ...

You see, many women grow up totally ignorant of cricket because they've never been introduced to its finer points. And isn't it so often the case that, having reached the age of

The original England ladies' cricket team.

maturity, such blissfully ignorant young maidens then compound the problem by falling head over heels in love with an ardent cricketer. All the little things that the cricketer has simply taken for granted become 'double dutch' to his new love. It can take a long and patient period of indoctrination to rectify. Take the case of one first-class cricketer who went to his new girlfriend's home after a particularly disappointing day's play.

'How did you go today, Darling?' she asked, bubbling with interest as he crossed the threshhold.

'Rotten,' replied the player, 'run out for a duck.' His lady friend was determined to be supportive.

'What a terrible shame,' she said, 'was it a good ball?'

Once cricket is in your blood, that's where it stays. Cyril Allcott began his first-class career in New Zealand playing for Hawke's Bay in the 1920–21 season. Eleven years later he announced his retirement from first-class cricket after playing the final Test against H.B. Cameron's South African tourists in 1931–32. But Allcott was to play one more first-class match — 14 seasons later at the age of 49 — when he was picked to play for Otago against Auckland! In Auckland's first innings he took three wickets, though he bowled under the handicap of an injured foot after being hit there when out lbw to a fast bowler. A press report of the game summed up the passing of the years.

'His bowling was of a good length and he could gain turn, but much of this was nullified through his slower pace since he played in Auckland *14 seasons ago.*'

Just prior to the 1980–81 season, the Australian Cricket Board produced a Code of Behaviour in a bid to smarten players' demeanour on and off the field in Sheffield Shield games. A string of acts that certainly *weren't cricket* during previous seasons had brought about the Board's move and it seemed to put a stopper on the matter. Indeed, it wasn't until the second last weekend of the Shield season that umpires during a game between NSW and WA in Perth saw fit to register the first charges under the Code.

West Australian wicketkeeper Rod Marsh was the first named after he had hotly disputed an umpire's decision. Dennis Lillee's first delivery of the NSW first innings had gone sailing down leg side to the boundary and the umpire had called four byes (a signal which pricks the pride of every conscientious keeper) when most at the ground thought it should have been called four wides. In accordance with the Code of Behaviour, Marsh's case was heard by his WA teammates and they duly accepted the charge and fined him the minimum of $25. Marsh took this well enough. Then, when Lillee pitched an identical delivery in his first over of the second innings and the same umpire this time signalled four wides, Marsh showed there were no hard feelings by turning to the ump and clapping.

Later, on the same day, NSW batsman John Dyson fell foul of the umpires on a more serious offence when he kicked down his leg stump in disgust after having been given out, caught close-in off spinner Bruce Yardley. On this occasion the NSW team had to adjudicate. They accepted the charge, reprimanded Dyson and fined him $30. Of course the hearing took place behind closed doors, but it was revealed later that the NSW players had in fact held a mock trial. It had been felt that tangible evidence was needed before it could be proven that Dyson had, indeed, committed the offence. One of the wags in the side went to some trouble to produce a stump with, drawn on it, a right boot mark. When the stump was shown as 'Exhibit A' during the 'trial', the 'accused' was asked to examine it and verify that it was, in fact, the stump involved in the incident. Sharp-eyed Dyson, on inspecting the stump, rose to ask the 'court' to dismiss the case. The stump showed a right boot mark, he said, and he reminded them that he had kicked *his* stump down with his left boot!

You can't always judge a book by its cover, can you? An article in the New Zealand Herald previewing a match in Auckland between Auckland and Canterbury way back in 1877–78 was unstinting in its praise of the work done by the groundsman. 'A really good wicket has been prepared by Mr Yates,' went the report, 'such a wicket as few who could hold a bat could help scoring on...' What that in mind it was strange, to say the very least, that Auckland were bowled out in the fourth innings of the match for only 13 runs in just 38 minutes. And that innings still stands as the lowest score on record in New Zealand first-class cricket history. Perhaps the weather had something to do with it all — a contemporary report on how the game went indicates that it rained so heavily on the first day that the luncheon tent was washed away!

Cricket in Australia and the name Alan McGilvray are almost synonymous ... they even wrote a song about the doyen of radio broadcasters, which claimed that 'The game is not the same without McGilvray'. His association with the game goes back many, many years to the days when he was captain of New South Wales for a brief period. He figured in the pioneering of the radio coverage of cricket with the introduction of 'synthetic broadcasts', a system used before direct broadcasting was possible. Cables from London were received in Sydney and the radio commentators made up their own story, complete with sound effects, from those few lines. Since those days things have improved for 'Mac' and he now covers Test matches all over the world in relative comfort and using the latest electronic equipment.

His long association with the game has been recognised by the Queen, with an MBE, and the Australian Government, with the Order of Australia. During the receipt of the latter, at Government House in Sydney, Mac became a little confused with the very precise instructions recipients were given by the aides concerning where to stand, which foot to lead off with when called and how many steps to take before reaching the presentation point. As the person ahead of him was being decorated by the Governor, Mac anticipated the take-off time and took half a step forward but he was pulled up short when an aide whispered sharply, 'Not yet!' When finally arrived at the duly appointed time and place the Governor, Sir Roden Cutler, a fanatical follower of the game and an old friend, said as he reached forward to pin on the medal, 'Might have been "no-balled" for over-stepping there, Mac!'

South Australia were playing Victoria at the Adelaide Oval during the 1980–81 season when one of the visiting team, the giant frame of Gary Cosier, made a sudden exit from the field. After a brief delay the twelfth man dashed down the stairs to take up his duties and enable the game to proceed. When one of the wags in the 'garden seats' by the boundary in front of the members' stand saw the tiny figure of Graham Matthews jog past on to the ground he complained loudly: 'That's half of him replaced. Now where's the other ten stone?'

When Dennis Lillee was at his peak in the early and middle 1970s, his sheer speed was enough to put a falter in the step of the best batsmen in the world. As the years passed he naturally slowed down a little but brought more of the finer points of bowling, such as swing and cut, into his game. Even so, he was quick enough for most and retained the ability to throw in the occasional scorcher, just to let them know it was still there. Umpire Robin Bailhache tells the story of the Demon toiling away with little help from a pretty flat wicket in the First Test against the West Indies at the Brisbane Cricket Ground in 1979–80. It was hot, frustrating toil for a bowler of Lillee's type, recalls Bailhache, and after a while the champion became a little worn and exasperated. At the end of one over a dejected Lillee stood halfway down the pitch and Bailhache moved to save him the walk back to get his hat. As he handed it over, a rather haggard-looking Lillee said:

'Jeez, it's hard being a fast bowler and I ought to know ... I used to be one!'

After giving Australia a five-one hiding in the 1978–79 series, England toured again the following summer in a campaign that was shared with the West Indies. The Australian side was then back to full-strength after the com-

promise between World Series Cricket and the Australian Cricket Board and the boot was well and truly on the other foot as a England struggled throughout the series and were soundly beaten in each of the three Tests. Australia were putting the finishing touches on the last of those victories when a wag in outer at the Melbourne Cricket Ground poured some salt in the gaping wounds.

'There's only three things wrong with you Poms,' he shouted, 'you're overpaid, over-rated and over 'ere.'

Rod Marsh usually looks on the brighter side of things. A wicked sense of humour has always made him the life of the party in dressingroom situations. His positive philosophy was never more tested than when the burly youngster was dismissed for a 'duck' in the first innings of his second first-class game in Western Australia. In his first game the week before (for WA against the West Indies in the 1968-69 season) Marsh, picked as a batsman only made nought in the first innings and 104 in the second. Though others might hang their heads in such a situation, Marsh had different thoughts as he unbuckled his pads after that second duck (when playing for a Combined XI against the West Indies).

'It really isn't such a bad game,' he said to himself, 'I mean, 0, 104, 0 ... the way things are going I'll average fifty for my career and that can't be bad.'

Talking about cricketers with a sense of humour, what about Doug Walters? Rod Marsh's first Test match was against England in Brisbane at the start of the 1970-71 series and the West Australian's selection had been controversial, to say the least. The Eastern States press had been a strong lobby for the retention of Walters' New South Wales team-mate and good friend Brian Taber. The England first innings began on the second day and not long before stumps Marsh had his first victim, the prized wicket of Boycott. Though reasonably happy that night, he was absolutely devastated early the following day when he dropped sharp chances off Edrich, Fletcher and d'Oliveira. He eventually added the scalps of Fletcher, Illingworth and Snow to his earlier catch, giving him four for the innings, but those three misses haunted him. Walters must have sensed this when they were having a beer after play:

'Never mind Bacchus,' he said, 'if you'd caught them all you'd have had a world record in your first innings!'

Captains *can* have their problems ...

Over the good number of years he has been playing first-class cricket, Rod Marsh has become known as one of the game's great extroverts. His every act as a wicketkeeper and a hard-hitting batsman breathes expression — and, either on or off the field, he's invariably in the thick of things. Indeed, it could be said that he's never stuck for a word. Well, *rarely* stuck for a word! There was just one day. It was during one of his first games as captain of the West Australian side in the 1975–76 season.

He was addressing his team, all of whom had gathered enthusiastically round their leader in the dressingroom, before they were to take the field after the luncheon adjournment. Rod had obviously spent the latter part of the interval planning some words of encouragement and motivation because when the moment came to speak, he was full of fire.

'Now listen to me, you bastards,' he said, with typical Marsh bluntness, 'I've got just three things to say to you ... for God's sake, you bowlers, bowl to your fields — and you fieldsmen, give it all you've got. We can knock these swines over in no time and be back here with our feet up. Let's go and give it to 'em.' And he headed for the door.

Australi

...eper John MacLean at work (1978–79 Test series v England).

He hadn't taken more than a couple of strides when Ric Charlesworth, one of the more astute (and obviously less bedazzled) members of the WA line-up, chimed in.

'Hey skipper,' he said, 'what about the *third* thing you were going to say to us?' The solid frame of Marsh froze mid-stride.

'The third thing ...' he muttered gruffly, '... the third thing ... Oh, bugger it, I've forgotten ... let's go, anyway.'

There was angry talk about the state of the Melbourne Cricket Ground wicket before and during the Third Test against Pakistan in the 1981-82 season. Australian captain Greg Chappell, who led the cavalry charge, even urged that the forthcoming First Test against the West Indies be moved to another ground in the interests of cricket. Yet despite the wailings, the wicket for the Pakistan match could not have been too bad. The tourists declared as 8 for 500 and Graeme Wood was able to score a century for the home side. However, Australia was forced to follow-on; failed again in the second innings; and lost by an innings and plenty. Some blamed the wicket. 'Well,' said one of the pundits, 'there weren't many dismissals I saw that could be blamed on the wicket.'

'Except for Allan Border, who was run-out so cheaply in each innings,' replied another. 'He could certainly blame the wicket for being too bloody long both times!'

Graham McKenzie found himself in a bit of a pickle when he was suddenly thrown into the role of Australian captain during a Test in England on the 1968 tour. Regular captain Bill Lawry and vice-captain Barry Jarman were indisposed and McKenzie had to step into the breech at a moment's notice. It was quite a number of years since the big fast bowler had captained any cricket team at all. Well, he led the players out on to the field quite handsomely, but then it all fell apart. McKenzie's normal job when Australia went on the field in a Test match was to take the new cherry, measure out his run and get stuck into the batsmen with single-minded purpose. So he did just that. He had taken a couple of strides in his run-up for the first delivery before he saw to his horror nine fieldsmen and a wicketkeeper standing in a group at the other end — waiting for their new leader to despatch them to their positions!

In Sydney it's the Hill, in Melbourne it's Bay 13 in the Southern Stand, in Adelaide and Brisbane, the Scoreboard Mound, in Perth it's simply The Outer. These are the sections of various first-class cricket venues around Australia where the most spirited barrackers congregate — there a beer, a bugle, and a bloody good voice are, if anything, more important than a well-executed cover drive.

It was in the outer or southern or river end of the WACA Ground in Perth one warm Sunday afternoon where the first chant of 'Li-lee ... Li-lee ... Li-lee ' was contrived to give heart to the local hero. That was in the middle 1970s. The message spread like wildfire. Soon the wailing cry echoed wherever the demon bowler was seen streaming in to let fly his thunder-balls. It has even been heard on grounds in England.

Doubtless the eternal cry gave fire to Dennis Lillee's ego time and time again, inspiring a thrust from the champion that might otherwise have been saved for another day. But what of the boys in the outer at the WACA Ground when their idol made his first appearance back home after having broken Richie Benaud's Australian Test wicket-taking record in the final Test against India late in the summer of 1980–81? As Lillee raced to figures of three-for-four off five overs in the McDonald's Cup semi-final against Victoria, a new chant began (to the tune of the Christmas Carol 'Deck the halls with boughs of holly, fa-la-la-la-etc'):

'Dennis Lillee walks on water, fa-la-la-la etc'.

And the way he was bowling he just about could!

Fiery Freddie Trueman was not only a marvellously well equipped fast bowler — figures of 307 wickets from his 67 Test appearances tell the story — but he was also a fearsome sight when tearing in to deliver the ball. His burly frame, the mop of black hair that always seemed to whip across his face as he let one fly and, perhaps worst of all, the eternal Trueman scowl. All combined to wreak havoc among the faint of heart. The apparition was fierce enough to make a few sitting in the first row on the safe side of the fence shudder.

So it was not surprising that when the Indian team toured England in 1952 and found that they were up against this new firebrand from Yorkshire in the Tests, that their stamina was put to the ultimate stress. In fact the young Trueman in his first series claimed an amazing twenty-nine victims from just four Tests played. The story has it that by the end of the tour it was nothing for a group of Indian batsman on seeing Freddie to greet him with a smile, a hint of a bow and a nervous chorus:

'Good morning, Mr Trueman!'

History shows that it's not that unusual for a batsman to score a 'five'. Occasionally the wide expanses of the Melbourne Cricket Ground or the extraordinarily-long straight hit of the Adelaide Oval will enable a fleet-of-foot pair to make them 'all-run'. But the most common method of adding five to your score in one fell hit is to acquire four of them on the overthrows of an overexcited fieldsman. By this method it is not unheard of for even a six to be scored.

But the unthinkable happened on the afternoon of the final day of the Third Test between Australia and New Zealand at the MCG in the 1980–81 season. Kiwi opener John Wright picked up an 'eight'! Wright played a delivery from Len Pascoe away to the deeps at square leg and he and Geoff Howarth were scrambling the fourth as the return came to 'keeper Rod Marsh, whose powerful throw at the bowler's end stumps went through to the long-on boundary. Wright was all smiles as his score moved from 19 to 27 ... big Len Pascoe was not.

West Australian batsman Greg Shipperd must rank among the shortest men to play first-class cricket. Watching him from the boundary, it even seems that his little legs are on the short side in comparison with the rest of his body. That may be more an error of perspective but Shipperd really does have very short legs. One commentator (off-air at the WACA Ground in Perth during a Sheffield Shield game) was more than somewhat fascinated by the proportions. After Shipperd had furiously scampered through for a snappy two, the broadcaster drily commented:

'You know, he takes seventy-two steps every time he runs up the wicket ...' he paused, then added, equally drily, '... in fact, a black tracker following his footsteps through the outback would probably say "four people"!'

Sunil Gavaskar's 1980–81 Australian touring team made their first landfall at Perth, right in the middle of a heatwave. Naturally the Indians shrugged off the heat. They were at the WACA practice nets every day as they worked hard to get acclimatised and find form on the faster, bouncier Australian wickets. But one problem wasn't so easy to shrug off — the swarms of flies that the hot spell produced.

The tourists tried to keep the flies off their faces by wearing handkerchieves in the style of masked bandits of old Western movies. This appealed to the press photographers but the last word on the matter came from the sole Indian journalist with the team at that early stage. He was asked, tongue in cheek, if the Indian players found the flavour of the West Australian flies repugnant. Straight as a dye the little Indian pressman replied:

'It's not so much the taste, but you must remember we have vegetarians in the party.'

The Northerner in England has a dry-as-chips humour. One was once overheard saying to another, 'Ee, yon bugger's a bit dour ... t' only time I ever saw 'im laff was when 'is wife broke 'er leg!' This ability to see a humorous twist in misfortune was evident in a home game at the Bacup club in the Lancashire League in the summer of 1980. Bacup, one of the small-town clubs with more downs than ups in its long career with the league, was having a good season for once, which attracted a good crowd for a vital clash late in the season. The perimeter of the Lanehead Ground was surrounded by parked cars and people as Bacup toiled to defeat Ramsbottom and maintain their proximity to the top of the table. In the limited overs League games there are a certain number of points available for a win — plus a bonus point if a side bowls out the opposition in achieving that victory.

Bacup batted first and after a while it became obvious they were going to restrict Ramsbottom to a score below their own. But captain Roger Law was desperate for that extra point, so he brought spinner 'Kes' into the attack to lob up some juicy deliveries in an effort to buy the last couple of wickets.

When the Bacup followers realised that Law was risking the main win points in pursuit of the bonus point, quite a few

ribald calls flew across the ground. Still Law persisted with Kes and finally a burly tailender cottoned on to one of his floaters and banged it straight through the windscreen of a car at the boundary. Bacup went on to win and as Law was walking from the changerooms to the social club, he passed the car with the broken windscreen. Its owner was inside, head down, cleaning up the mess.

'Are ya reet, Ted?' asked Roger. Ted's ruddy face, with flat cap on top, poked through the gaping hole in the windscreen.

'Reet!' he exclaimed loudly. 'Didn't you 'ear me ... three times ah towd thee to tak yon bugger off.'

Comes the day in every cricketer's career when he starts asking his body to do things of which it is no longer capable. That's the time when fast bowlers turn to spin and suddenly realise that they can bat a whole lot better than they had ever imagined. It is also the time when opening batsmen drop down the order with the rationale that their experience will help bolster the tail. That's the time when outfielders begin to apply themselves assiduously to slips catching practice and over a beer start trying to convince the captain they'd make darned good close-to-the-wicket fieldsmen — especially with a third man out to overcome the problems involved in a chase. One of the first areas to go, it seems is the ageing cricketer's throwing arm. What used to be a pick-up-and-throw in the one motion becomes a laboured process, first in the bending down and second with keeping to a minimum the strides required to load up and get the throw away. One cricketer in the twilight of a valuable career summed it all up this way, 'My one remaining ambition is to be able to throw four overthrows!'

The elegant stokeplay and the gazelle-like movements in the

cover of the Victorian Paul Sheahan gave pleasure to a lot of cricket lovers. In fact his career, which spanned 31 Tests for 1594 runs at 33.91 and included two centuries, was considered by many to have been nipped in the bud when he retired to concentrate on a teaching career. Not so the miserable columnist for an Australian girlie magazine who had nothing better to do than to pick a team comprising the 'worst' players ever to pull on the baggy green cap. For this infamous line-up included Sheahan, of all people! But, as the quick-witted Victorian later pointed out, it's far better to be talked about in any light than never to be talked about at all.

Anyway, Sheahan does admit to having had a most wretched tour of England in 1972. He recalls going into the game against Sussex at Hove before the fourth Test sorely out of form and badly needing runs. When he reached the crease wondering where his next run might come from, he saw the reassuring figure of his Victorian teammate Keith Stackpole propped on his bat at the other end. England's Test fast bowler John Snow was to send the first ball to Sheahan which, as he puts it, made him even keener to get off the mark and get down the other end for a bit of a breather.

Snow's first delivery was well up on the leg stump and Sheahan pushed it wide of mid-on, screamed 'Yes' and put his head down to sprint the 22 yards to safety. It was always going to be a close go for his mate Stacky, who had to run to the danger end, but Victorians have been known to always stick together and reluctantly he took off. After going a few strides Sheahan looked up to see the tall, lanky figure of Tony Greig making excellent ground to his right at mid-on and about to apply his great reach to drop on the ball. Sensing that real problems confronted his partner, Sheahan switched his eyes to the retreating rear of Stacky, legs pumping and broad buttocks rotating furiously as he frantically tried to bridge the gap between himself and the crease. From his viewpoint Sheahan could see to his dismay that it really was going to be nip and tuck ... away went Greig's throw and to Sheahan's horror it broke the stumps with his mate sprawling in most ungainly fashion — seemingly a fraction short. As Sheahan's smote his forehead in horror, the Sussex appeal for the run-out was greeted by a bold 'Not out' from the square leg umpire, an expatriate Australian called Cec Pepper, who had turned to umpiring when his days as a professional in the Lancashire leagues were over.

Apart from being a very fine all-rounder in his day,'Pep' was known to all as a character who invariably had a few words to say. Stackpole couldn't believe his good fortune and was trying to regain his composure as Pep jogged in to remake the stumps. As he placed the bails in position, the umpire muttered out of the corner of his mouth. 'If it had been anybody but that Tony Greig it might have gone the other way,' he said with a twinkle in his eye. 'Course it might not have too,' he added with a chuckle.

When the eighth wicket fell in the second innings of the Plunkett Shield game between Central Districts and Otago at Dunedin during the 1952-3 season, the Otago opening batsmen could have been excused for beginning their mental preparation for an innings surely soon to begin. At one end of the wicket was Ian Leggat an all-rounder who had a career aggregate to that time of 113 runs from 12 innings ... and joining him at the other end was medium-pace bowler Harry Cave, whose 40 in the first innings of that match was the highest score of his 43-game first-class career to date. But the two players, both of whom went on to play for New Zealand (Cave making 19 appearances and Leggat just the one), were purposeful in their resolve to buck the odds and fight a worthwhile rearguard action.

When some time later Cave was finally dismissed and the stand at last broken, a New Zealand record ninth-wicket

The 'Big Ship' Warwick Armstrong practicing at Lords.

partnership of 239 had been posted. Cave finished with 118 and his partner 142 not out — not bad for a couple of rabbits!

The Indian touring party in Australia for the 1980–81 season included three players who, standing on their tip-toes, still wouldn't go within a bull's roar of shoulder height to the giant West Indian Joel 'Big Bird' Garner. Reading from the tallest to shortest, the Indian trio would line up: Yashpal Sharma, Sunil Gavaskar and his brother-in-law Gundappa Viswanath — with none of them much over five feet.

Surely 'Vishy' would go awfully close to being the shortest Test cricketer in history, a fact which has inspired many jokes over the years. Like the time during the Second Test in Adelaide on that tour when a white washer hat flew from the crowd in a gust wind and came to rest flat on the ground as Shivlal Yadav was bowling to Kim Hughes in melting heat. The sight of the hat at deep extra cover rather tickled Rod Marsh's fancy as he sat in the player's viewing area. He called his mate Dennis Lillee from the depths of the dressing-room at the rear.

'Hey Fot,' he said, pointing at the hat on the ground, 'have a look at Vishy out there at extra — the little bugger's not even moving in with the bowler!'

Many a better batsman than Ashley Mallett has been put to fright by Dennis Lillee storming in from back near the sight-board and flinging down a thunderbolt. For example, when England toured Australia in 1974–75 such was the combined effect of Lillee and Jeff Thomson that it was said of more than one of their batsmen as he came to the crease, 'There goes a man who can think of at least five thousand places he'd rather be than where he is right now.' And who could blame batsmen for being phased by such a relentless barrage

66

of pace?

Certainly not Ashley Mallett, who has never been all that fond of the quick stuff. Well, WA were playing South Australia at the Adelaide Oval in the mid-1970s and there was poor old 'Rowdy' facing a fiery Lillee. To give Mallett his credit, he got behind the first couple. He took the first in the rib cage. The second smashed into his gloves, whereupon he threw his bat and gloves to the ground and put on quite a song and dance. When finally he could be encouraged to retrieve his equipment, replace the gloves and rejoin the battle, it was obvious to those nearby that he no longer had any stomach for it. Still he took his stance, albeit a little gingerly, and waited.

Lillee streaked in to deliver the killer blow, but by the time he reached a couple of paces short of the delivery stride it had become too much for Rowdy. He stood away quickly, raising his left hand, and Lillee had to abort in the delivery stride — a happening that far from pleases a fast bowler, which the Demon told him in no uncertain terms. Behind the stumps, WA captain Rod Marsh was not amused, either. He dashed up to Mallett and gave him a terrible mouthful, adding:

'Don't you ever do that to my fast bowler again.' While all this transpired, Mallett was frantically trying to collect his composure a little and gather what was left of his thoughts.

'Oh,' he stammered, still waving his left hand and trying desperately to sound cool, 'I only wanted the sightscreen moved.'

That was Rowdy's last straw ... you see, he'd played at the Adelaide Oval long enough to know that the sightscreens there are bolted to big uprights in the ground. They can't be moved!

The summer of 1980–81 will surely go down as the 'season to forget' for harrassed members of the Melbourne Cricket

Club hierarchy. That was when the spotlight fell on the wicket square at the club's famous headquarters, the Melbourne Cricket Ground. The wicket played so atrociously for most of the season that Australian captain Greg Chappell led a mounting chorus of criticism for its barren, unpredictable surface. As official concern grew, emergency meetings were held between the club and the Victorian Cricket Association, which hires the ground for major matches. As a result, thousands of small circular plugs of new grass were planted in the sizable bare patches, giving the whole square a polka-dot effect. However, there just wasn't enough time for the grass to cover sufficiently and in the end commonsense prevailed; the final two first-class fixtures of the season were scheduled instead for Kardinia Park in Geelong.

Of course, the MCG wicket was most under the microscope in the days leading up to, and during, the two Test matches played there that season — particularly the second, which was the Third Test against India in February. By that time the little plugs of grass had taken grip and officials, hoping against all odds that a better wicket would result, resisted pressure to have the Test venue changed.

So much had been said and written about the strip that it was no surprise to see press, radio and television men poring over the 22-yards on the morning of the first day's play. They found something of a patchwork quilt with the polka-dot pattern of the plugs of grass coming through strongly. So, too, did officials from the Melbourne club, the Victorian association and the Australian Cricket Board, also taking a nervous last-minute look at the wicket. It was one of the latter band who saw the lighter side of it all when he called across to one of the media men giving the surface the once over:

'Looks like it's got a good dose of the measles, doesn't it?'

One of the more interesting sidelights to recent Test matches at the Melbourne Cricket Ground has been a competition among spectators for the best banner displayed around the ground. The result has been a lot of fun and, no doubt, a few headaches for the judges because of the generally high standard. The inaugural contest was won by wit who displayed what must have been an outsized double bed sheet with a simple monogram: 'Bill Lawry's handkerchief'. So much for the proportions of the former Australian captain's proboscis! The eye-catcher at the Australia-New Zealand Test at the MCG over Christmas, 1980, made a more political comment. Following hard on the heels of the first and second Tests between the two countries, both of which were over in three days, the poster read, 'All we want for Xmas is a five-day Test'. Perhaps an Australian Cricket Board entry? And, one which must have tickled the fancy of the locals, poked a little fun at one of their idols, who never had been all that sharp in the field but had been seen in the covers (of all places) quite regularly in the first two Tests. It read simply, 'Jim Higgs loves Miss Fielding'. The Third Test in the other series of that summer, between Australia and India, was played at th MCG and one prominently-displayed sign summed up the tourists' batting woes in this manner, 'You Indians eat a lot of curry ... why don't you get the runs?'

There was something special about the way Les Favell used to play cricket. Untamed aggression and a deep well of self-confidence enabled him to float through a long career as an opening batsman for South Australia and, occasionally, Australia. The little power-pack was a down-to-earth man who played his cricket the same way. It was not unusual to see Favell belt the very first ball of a match, hurled down by the fastest of bowlers, straight back past the hapless fellow

See over: Kalgoorlie cricket team of 1896!

71

lot.' In fact, Favell could often be heard talking to himself or to his batting partner as he banged the ball away to one part or another. One of his favourite strokes was the hook and many's the time he was heard shouting as he laid back to despatch a short one with typical fury, 'Happy Birthday, Les', or, as it went scorching off the middle, 'Don't bother running, son, that's four!'

The 1980–81 World Series Cup one-day series involving Australia, New Zealand and India produced some high-quality cricket of its kind. Close games abounded. The series also produced some excellent individual performances and few were more regularly in that picture than the great New Zealand quickie, Richard Hadlee. The tall Kiwi really had a field day during the fifth qualifying game, against India at the WACA Ground in Perth. He claimed the wicket of Indian master batsman Sunil Gavaskar with his very first ball and ended up with 5–32 from nine overs to rightly be rewarded with man-of-the-match. The remarkable thing about Hadlee's bowling that day was that his first four wickets fell from the first delivery of a new spell — he had to wait a couple of overs for victim No. 5! Despite Hadlee's brilliance, New Zealand lost the game by five runs and stand-in captain Mark Burgess later was full of self-recriminations.

'It was rank bad captaincy by me,' he said, with something of a grin, 'when Richard took that fourth wicket with the first ball of his fourth spell, I should have taken him off straight away and kept the sequence going. We would have had them out far quicker than we eventually did.'

Surely Jack D'Arcy, the former New Zealand Test batsman, could have claimed some sort of a record! D'Arcy was a real man on the move, so much so that in each of three successive appearances in the local Plunkett Shield competition he played for a different team. Here's how it worked out: He played for Canterbury against Auckland in the 1958-59 season; next he appeared for Wellington against Canterbury during 1959-60; and the following season he stripped for Otago against Canterbury. He actually appeared in a first-class game for South Island in between, so making it four different teams in successive matches. Phew!

When New South Wales played Victoria at the Sydney Cricket Ground during the 1980-81, season, the home side were looking for a draw to deny the Victorians any outright points and thus consolidate their position at the top of the Sheffield Shield table. So, for the most part, the game deteriorated into a boring snail-crawl. In one particularly dull period of play the sightboard attendant at the northern end of the ground nodded off. He was soon fast asleep in his chair at his post, a lapse which could be excused in the circumstances.

However, just at that time the NSW quickie Lenny Pascoe decided to change his approach and bowl round the wicket. Naturally the Victorian batsman wanted the sightboard moved to accommodate the switch. Then the problems began for the slumbering sightscreen man. He didn't see the umpire signal a change was needed. He was in fact so far off in the land of nod that he didn't even hear the calls which increased to bellows. Finally Pascoe, who had been standing near the top of his mark, rolled the ball along the ground at him. The ball struck the attendant on the foot and woke him. He had, however, been sitting with one leg across the other, restrictive the blood flow, and the limb had 'gone to sleep'. So when he tried to spring to action he fell flat on his face on the turf. With players and spectators in fits of laughter, the attendant tried again and again to get up, but failed. Then Pascoe came to the rescue. He sprinted to the sightboard, helped the embarrassed attendant back into his chair then moved the board himself at the directions of a chortling batsman. And the game went on.

At the head of the Australian attack in the 1930s was a tall, lithe speedster called Ernie McCormick, who played twelve Tests before the World War. Just before the conflict, Don Bradman's Australians toured England and big Ernie was a member of the party. Ernie, who has become known as quite a wag among the regulars in the Long Room at the Melbourne Cricket Ground, tells the story about the Australians' game against Worcestershire on that tour:

'I was bowling pretty quick and one got up a bit and hit a fellow called Berry on the head,' says Ernie. 'He wasn't too good and had to be carted off to hospital for observation. The following day-off, most of the Aussies went to an air pageant being held nearby. While we were there I was introduced to Berry's charming wife. I felt terrible about what had happened and apologised profusely to the good lady, but I wasn't ready for the reply:

"Oh don't worry," she said, "I've been wanting to do that for years and years".'

Out of the mouths of babes ... a discussion overheard between a group of young teenagers during a train ride to the Melbourne Cricket Ground for the Test between Australia and India in 1980–81. The lads were obviously quite excited about the action that lay ahead in a day at the big cricket. But it certainly wasn't all too much for one, who felt the occasion warranted a little philosophy. Succinctly he summed up the changes that had come over the great game of cricket in recent years:

'Haven't things altered,' he told his mate, 'in the old days you'd sit on a seat and clap and say "Well played" — now we stand on the seat and scream as loud as we can whenever anything happens.'

WA and Queensland went into the final Sheffield Shield game of the 1980–81 season virtually on a winner-take-all basis. WA ended up outpointing Queensland and winning the Shield, thanks largely to a magnificent fighting 140 from diminutive batsman Greg Shipperd, who was named man-of-the-match. However, to most people the turning point of the game came soon after the start of the Queensland first innings, which followed Shipperd's marathon performance. In a blistering spell of four deliveries in his fourth over, Dennis Lillee sent Queensland batting mainstays Kepler Wessels and Greg Chappell (for a duck) back to the pavilion. Lillee was on fire.

Before beginning his fifth over, which he was to bowl to Allan Border, Lillee took time arranging an almost-ridiculously attacking field. After much gesticulating and hair-pulling he convinced captain Kim Hughes, way in the distance in the slips area, to bring the man at fine leg up to a leg gully to join the silly mid-on. Then he fast-talked Hughes into bringing the man at cover into a cordon of five slips and two gullies. Not a man out of the close catching positions: not a man in front of the wicket on the off side. As this intimidating field settled into place and the King stood surveying the scene from the top of his mark, a voice wailed from the outer:

'Put the bloody umpire in at silly mid-off, Fot.'

A good many years ago, when not many people had vehicles, a young cricketer was picked up and given a lift by a man in a chauffeur-driven limousine. The cricketer didn't seem to be too happy and his host asked him what was wrong.

'I've had a terrible day at cricket,' he said, 'I dropped three catches and made a duck.'

The man asked his driver to go off course and take the unhappy cricketer to his home. The next week the same thing happened... the same car came along and the cricketer again accepted a lift. Once more he was morose and, on being questioned, admitted that again he'd had a rotten day on the field — no runs and more dropped catches. This time the owner of the car was in a hurry to get home, but he instructed the driver to drop him off and then take the young fellow to his home. Incredibly, the following weekend the car was going along the same road when the owner spotted the young cricketer again and told the driver to pull up. As he wound down the window to offer the lad a ride, the cricketer's sad face turned hostile.

'Get lost,' he spat out, 'you're bringing me bad luck.'

When the ABC's Perth commentary team were sizing up their new broadcast box — a glass-fronted room mounted directly above the sightscreen at the southern end of the ground — there was considerable speculation about the chances of a ball being hit into their laps.

Nobody hit one anywhere near the box until the very last game of the season, when cavalier batsman Bruce Yardley cut loose and sent one sailing high in the direction of the glass front of the ABC box. Dennis Cometti was in the ball-by-ball commentators's seat at the time and, with the ball coming straight at him, he stood up at the ready and announced to his listeners:

'Excuse me, but I'm about to take a catch!'

The ball in fact dropped just short of the window and special comments man Norm O'Neill was moved to comment:

'This big-hitting will be really taking the shine off the ball.'

Replied Cometti: 'Oh, I don't know... it looked in pretty good nick to me!'

Lillee found himself in trouble with the law at the end of a trip to Adelaide with the WA team. He and Rod Marsh had been lent a car for the duration and were in a mad hurry to return it before dashing to the airport to fly home. To save time circling the block in the heavy traffic, Lillee drove a few metres the wrong way up a one-way road and ducked into the car yard. This transgression had been noted by a motorcycle patrolman, who had pulled alongside the car and drawn his notebook before Lillee and even turned off the ignition. According to Marsh, the officer proceeded to tear Lillee to shreds for 'irresponsible driving'. The champion quickie sat as meekly as a lamb and took the lambasting squarely on the chin. The patrolman then pocketed his notebook and kicked his machine over, adding with a snarl:

'I'm letting you off with a warning, but next time you're in Adelaide, Mister Lillee ... (pregnant pause and a noticeable shudder from the demon bowler) ... you'd better give those West Indies a bloody hiding.'

Exit the law wearing a toothy grin.

Surely there are no more dyed-in-the-wool cricket fanciers than the English. Their country is the birthplace and home of cricket. Almost to a man they look upon the game as a heritage, to be adored by players, spectators or just casual observers. It blooms each summer weekend throughout the length and breadth of the country. Countless games, are contested with similar zeal, whether Test matches or County games, club encounters or village green affairs. There may not be much rib-tickling humour at the top end of the scale, but down on the village greens it's often a case of fun and games, particularly when it's a 'beer match'. Such an occasion is the annual clash between the Lollards and the Davenant Society, two groups within Lincoln College, one of the thirty-plus colleges which make up the famous Oxford University.

This is a beer match with, well, a difference. Each player *must* carry pint pot. These receptacles, which must accompany the player wherever he goes on the field, are kept constantly filled by two rather serious freshmen undergraduates, garbed in ill-fitting tails and toting huge enamel jugs. Essentially, it is a game of cricket, but the rules are different. Acts of 'gross competence', like scoring a well-hit four, bowling somebody out or taking a catch, are inclined to bring a general cry of 'pint!' upon the player responsible. He must respond by downing a pint of beer in a gulp. A batsman whose competence permits him to scale the heights of double figures automatically reaches for his pot, which is strategically placed behind the stumps. Each time he scores five more runs there is a mandatory half-pint penalty.

As is proper in cricket, the umpire is the sole adjudicator ... and in these matches his duties are far-reaching. For example, he must decide whether to respond to a call from members of the batting side waiting on the boundary. When one of their batsmen has been going for a while, or has been too stuffy, they raise a cry of 'Out pilcher, you've been in too long!' If the umpire agrees, it takes him only a ball or two to send the batsman on his way.

But the umpires agree that their most demanding duty is choosing the correct moment to call 'dead ants'. On hearing these words, usually shouted in the middle of a critical piece of play — like while the ball is in the air and a catch is immi-

79

CRICKET AWARDS

New Zeala:

Edgar, caught Marsh Bowled Lillee, Perth Test 1980-1.

nent — every man on the field must hit the ground, lie on his back and wave his arms and legs in the air like a dying ant. The last man to answer the umpire's call (you've guessed it) must down a pint. The final unwritten law is that these games must end in a tie and it's up to the umpires and all players to see it produced ... or else, as one, they all gulp down a pint as they stagger off.

Cricket was set upon by a brand new phenomenon in the mid-1970s. It was the 'streaker', the intoxicated extrovert male who shed his clothes to make a naked dash across the field, normally winning just enough money in bets to cover the fine he received in court the following day. After a while spectators grew weary of these clowns but during a Sheffield Shield game between Western Australia and South Australia at the WACA Ground in Perth, there was a 'streak' with a difference. A new strip-nightclub had just opened in Perth and as a publicity gimmick three of the strippers did a naked run down a busy shopping mall in the heart of the city during the Friday lunch hour. Then word leaked out that they planned to repeat their act during play at the cricket the following day.

One of those who were alerted to this possibility was the producer of the television coverage of the game. Before play started he carefully briefed his cameramen, detailing one with the task of locating the girls before they actually began their streak. This man was given instructions to let his camera rove among the crowd in between overs. The producer also gave instructions for one camera to remain on the pitch at all times, so the game could be referred to if and when the interruption occurred. The vigil was maintained throughout the day, but a disappointed crew went home that night without the promised action. But the producer received a tip that the strippers would now do their bit the following day, Sunday, and he alerted his cameramen once more the following morning.

Finally the between-overs man laid his camera on three husky men and three girls dressed in kaftans coming through the gate at the western end of the ground and it was agreed by the producer that these *had* to be the strippers. Sure enough, at the end of the over, off came the kaftans and the three jumped the fence and ran on to the ground. The commentators, who had agreed solemnly to hold their silence through it all, burst into uncontrollable laughter. All cameras were on the naked bodies and none remained on the pitch throughout the incident. One fleet-footed girl made it to the wicket and ran down the off-side, where Ian Chappell gestured rather crudely at her with the handle of his bat. The girl was finally apprehended at mid-on by two burly policemen and led towards the boundary at long-on. She happened to be carrying a T-shirt, which the policemen, in an act of admirable self-denial, ordered her to don — the trouble was, it was too short for modest coverage. All of this went 'live' through the ABC's cameras to a commercial station in Adelaide on a hook-up arrangement and it just wasn't cricket! Naturally there was much discussion among the crew in the bar after play and each had his bit to say about which of the three strippers he had fancied most. The favourite was a tall, willowy brunette — but those who had made that choice soon retracted when they read in the morning newspaper the next day that the tall brunette was in fact a man who had undergone a sex-change operation!

A significant proportion of those who have tried, reckon there's no worse job than selector for a sporting team. No matter what line-up you choose, there's always somebody who feels overlooked or hard done by. It takes a special type of courage to front up to a player who has lost his place or missed selection in a borderline decision. Of course, it's not always possible for selectors to fully explain their motives for choosing a certain player to do a certain job — even though the man's credentials didn't appear to justify his inclusion ahead of another. Abusive and even threatening letters and telephone calls are part and parcel of the existence of selectors for sports in the public eye. On top of the reactions of unhappy players, their relatives, friends and supporters, selectors in the 'major' sports must also endure the whimsical attacks of the critics. And in the days leading up to an important selection meeting they can't pick up a newspaper or turn on a radio or televsion set without being told by one 'expert' or another just whom they should select. And if they don't heed the critic's advice, woe-betide them if the team fails! So if you thought a selector's lot was not always a happy one, you'd be right.

However, three West Australian cricket selectors still get a good belly laugh about some 'advice' they received from one pundit before they were to name their team for the opening Sheffield Shield game of a season in the early 1970s. The critic wrote a well-reasoned story listing the twelve players he'd like to see represent the State. When they examined this list, the three selectors had to agree: It looked a marvellous line-up — beautifully balanced with plenty of batting depth and any amount of bowling — it was just too good to be true. Why hadn't we thought of that, they asked themselves. They were about to accept the critic's line-up as their own, when one demurred.

'Hang on a minute,' he said, took another peek at the list and then burst out laughing. It took the others some time to calm him enough for an explanation.

'Have a look at it,' he chortled, 'there's no bloody wicket-keeper!'

Yanchep Sun City Cricket Club, at the coastal resort town of Yancep some 80 kilometres north of Perth, has more than one 'official' self-appointed comedian-cum-raconteur. And, judging by the way most games are played at that centre, there may never be a shortage of material. But certainly the best opportunity is the annual 'test' match — a head-to-head confrontation between the Poms (English migrant fraternity in the settlement) and the Aussies (anybody born in Australia who cares to tear himself away from the Sunday session at the local). The winners of this bizarre sporting event (to use a phrase lightly) have their team name inscribed on an urn called the Embers. This specially-turned replica of the Ashes urn houses a capsule containing the ashes of the jock-strap worn by Derek Randall during the 1979–80 gargantua.

The 'test' produces one humorous happening after another as hands deft at pulling craypots and fishing lines (or lifting a beer glass) are turned not-so-deftly to the elegant art of cricket. During the 1980–81 conflict for the Embers one occurrence particularly tickled the palate of the raconteurs:

'It was like this,' one told a mate over a beer. 'There was big Mike way out in the deeps at square leg. And, boy,' as big Mike got a gut on 'im — all paid for, mind you, must be his biggest asset. 'E really is a mountain of a man. In fact, 'e's so bloody big and 'e weighs so bloody much that when 'e goes out to bat on one of them concrete wickets we've got to send out three other buggers with 'im to stand at the other end of the wicket in case the slab starts to sink at 'is end! Well, one of the lads belts one way up in the air and it flies out towards deep mid-wicket, not all that far from where big Mike's standin'. Quick as a flash Mike drops 'is can — without spilling' a drop, mind you — and off 'e goes after that motorin' missile. Fair surprises us all, Mike does, because 'e really gets goin' and covers quite a bit of ground tryin' to get under that flamin' thing. Well, 'e's just about to launch 'imself into a final effort to take the catch when 'e trips on a bit of rabbit diggin's — ground's a bit rough in some parts, you know. 'E 'its the ground, oh boy 'e 'its the ground. In fact, 'e 'its it so 'ard that the bloody number plates were 'eard rattlin' on the scoreboard some eighty metres away. Well, after the game we was at the pub drownin' our sorrows when one of the lads 'as a bright idea and rings the observatory down in Perth. There it was in black and white ... big Mike's fall and registered three on the Richter scale. Blimey!'

There are those among the cricket-playing fraternity who are inclined to treat fielding with scant regard for its importance in the game, an attitude that seems more prevalent among the younger group. Those who feel that way blithely play away their hours in the belief that only batting and bowling count. Nobody appreciates the folly of that attitude more than a bowler at the crease or a captain. Good catching and tight, pressure fielding are in fact the very essence of winning cricket.

This story, supposedly true, is about one captain's utter frustrations as he tried to get something out of a young team member whose attitude towards fielding was almost as abominable as his fielding technique. Night after night at practice he told the errant lad:

'Get your body behind the line of the ball, bend down as the ball arrives, get both hands behind it and keep both legs together.'

And he would add, 'Remember to do all those things and there'll be no misfields.'

However, on match days things never improved. After a month of perseverance the captain finally ran out of patience when the young fellow let three in a row go straight through his legs at mid-on. After the third miss and the subsequent

87

chase, when the fieldsman jogged back to his position he found his captain, red-faced with hands on hips waiting for him.

'Sorry skipper,' he mumbled, but it was too late.

'Sorry be dammed,' screamed the captain, 'you're not keeping your legs together like I told you ...' and then added ' ... and it's a bloody pity that twenty years ago your mother didn't do the same!'

'You can call me what you like so long as you don't call me late for breakfast.' This saying has its place, but not when it comes to visiting cricketers. Most radio and TV commentators take the pronunciation of cricketers' names seriously — as they should — and Indian teams have always provided a welter of tongue-twisters. In recent years the spinners Venkataraghavan and Chandrasekhar were so intimidating that the broadcasters were forced to compromise. They became Venkat and Chandra to everyone's relief — including the signwriters who had to paint their names for scoreboards around Australia.

Strangely, though, the name which caused the most confusion was that of Indian batsman Sunil Gavaskar. When the Indians toured Australia in 1977–78 broadcasters thought they'd sorted it out. All agreed that the correct pronunciation was G-V-AS-K-R. However, when the Indians returned for the summer of 1980–81 it wasn't quite so clear-cut. The tour began in Perth, where local broadcasters asked an Indian journalist with the team for some help with pronunciations. When it came to the team captain, Gavaskar, he advised: G-V-ARSK-R. Meanwhile another school of thought, fuelled by a rumour that it was supported by the man himself, had developed. This time it was GAV-S-KAR. Suddenly the issue was in complete confusion. So, on the eve of the first Test in Sydney, an ABC radio commentator tried to clear it up once and for all — right from the horse's mouth. To everyone's dismay, the ABC man found the definitive version completely different from the three in currency. It was GARV-S-K-R! This new twist caused such bedlam in the broadcast box, that the harrassed ABC man floundered on to another tack. Why not simply use his first name? After all, it was alright for Kapil Dev to be known simply as KARP-EEL, wasn't it? Just so. Now, how did one pronounce Gavaskar's first name? Said Gavaskar:

'Oh I don't mind SUNNY (his nickname), or SOON-IL or SOON-EEL or SUN-IL — but please don't give me SUNNY-HILL.' The band of now thoroughly befuddled broadcasters headed for the bar — to clear their heads.

Just about every cricket broadcaster has fiddled away time during a quiet period of play discussing the hordes of seagulls which invariably congregate at Australian cricket grounds. When a stroke carries the ball into a nestling gaggle of gulls, sending them soaring angrily into the air, it provides the commentators with a little embellishment for their talk. What can really get them talking is when a particularly fiercely struck ball hits a gull before it can move — as happened during the Adelaide Test between Australia and the West Indies in the 1979–80 season. The dazed bird was carried to the boundary by Dennis Lillee and placed in the care of a gentleman in the outer. This saga was strung out by the commentators until the bird had regained enough strength to fly off.

But have you ever wandered what induces hundreds of seagulls to fly in to cricket grounds during matches, when they're rarely sighted on other days? If it is the scavenging seagull's eternal hope of an easy meal, then why do they always settle so close to the wicket (and thus far from the crumbs of the crowd)? The great seagull question has been the subject of endless idle contemplation over many a cricket season, without substantial conclusions ever having been reached. That is, until a gentleman telephoned his local radio station in WA with the following:

'Seagulls are attracted to cricket matches by the tension generated by the players. Hence on days when there is no cricket, there are no seagulls either.'

Well, er ...? But then to reinforce his self-professed erudition on the subject, the gentleman became more expansive.

'What's more,' he said, 'the birds can anticipate bowling changes and move to safer positions prior to a new over.'

Well, I never ...

Whether it's our Cockney ancestry or whatever, Australians have become known for the use of rhyming slang. The art, if you call it that, has thrived over the years in the ranks of our cricketers. The game abounds with sayings such as 'Dorothy' (Dix) or 'Tom' (Mix) for a six, 'swiss-rolled' or 'rock 'n rolled' for bowled and so they go on. But picture, if you can, the Australian team going to England in the not-so-olden days by ship. The team's assistant-manager, a man of the world it's true but also a thoroughly well educated city accountant, bumped into one of his players in one of the corridors on the morning after a big, big night before. The assistant-manager could see at first glance that his man was far from well and asked the question, 'How're you going?' Came the groaned reply, 'Jeez I'm butcher's ... I've just put me onka down me nanny and had a Jimmy.' The assistant-manager scratched his balding pate as he moved to translate. After a few moments he came up with the solution. What the sick sailor had meant to say was, 'Jeez I'm unwell (butcher's hook — crook) ... I've just put my finger (onkaparinga) down my throat (nanny goat) and had a vomit (a Jimmy Burke).' 'Oh, I see,' said the assistant-manager as the player staggered off to his cabin. 'Somehow',' thought the bemused official, 'it didn't sound quite so bad untranslated.'

One of the highlights of the 1980–81 Australian cricket calender turned out to be a dinner at the Melbourne Cricket Club just before the last Test of the summer. It was held by the Crusaders, a band of mainly Victorian cricketers and cricket-lovers. The Crusaders' main occupation is playing matches against schools in and around Melbourne. At the head of this august band is an enthusiastic fellow known to all and sundry as 'Swan' Richards. Swan roped in as his permanent 12th-man, the Speaker of the House of Representatives, Sir Billy Snedden. And just to balance the political scales, he signed on Bob Hawke and Don Chipp for figurehead appointments. On the afternoon of the dinner a cricket match was played between the Politicians (including the three men mentioned, some other pollies *and* Tony Greig, Max Walker and Graham Yallop) and the Crusaders (the most notable of whom was Ian Chappell).

Guest speakers at the dinner, attended by a packed house of political, sporting and business notables, were the redoubtable Mr Hawke and former Test cricketer Paul Sheahan. These two had their work cut out for them, because they were preceded by an excellent toast to the Crusaders by leading cricket administrator Ray Steele and a memorable response from Swan Richards that was a grand blend of humour and pathos. What made Swan's speech all the more superb was, as pointed out by Ray Steele when proposing the toast, that the man had had more than his fair share of problems as a young lad. He had been unable to attend schools in the normal way things and at a very tender age had been given his chance in life when former Test player Barry Jarman agreed to give him fairly modest work in his Adelaide sports store business. Swan's enthusiasm, said Ray Steele, had carried him from one triumph to another, until he took control of operations at a prominent cricket bat maker's factory in the Melbourne suburbs.

Then Steele let the cat out of the bag in the origin of 'Swan' as his nickname. When Richards had played club cricket in Adelaide, his impetuous nature and unbridled enthusiasm had cost him dearly in his early days as a batsman. 'In fact,' said Steele, 'he was dismissed so many times without scoring that the term "duck" lost its significance. He was christened "Swan", which has stayed with him ever since.'

Dennis Lillee and Jeff Thomson between them wreaked fair havoc among England's batsmen during their 1974–75 tour of Australia. Their exploits in tandem really got the adrenallin pumping through the veins of a myriad of Australian supporters... and, it seems, the legion of journalists who followed the two teams around the country. One English journalist went to the trouble of listing the words pulled out of the thesaurus to describe the speed twins' work during one day of the Brisbane Test.

'They reveal,' wrote the journalist, 'that Thomson-Lillee's terrifying/lethal/hostile/fearsome/frightening/ferocious/blasting/blistering/dangerous/venemous/fierce/whirlwind/bullet-like bowling produced chilling/shivering/quivering/trembling/havoc among the English cricketers... in short, a feast of fiery fury.'

During this series the two Australian pacemen came in for their fair share of criticism for persistent short-pitched bowling. Lillee put his thoughts on the subject in a book he wrote called 'Back to the Mark', when he said: 'I bowl bouncers for one reason... to hit the batsman and thus intimidate him. I try to hit the batsman in the rib-cage when I bowl a pur-

poseful bouncer and I want it to hurt so much that the batsman won't want to face me any more.' On the same subject
Thommo was a little less forthright, but nevertheless showed
he felt a little the same way: 'You've got to make the batsman play at the ball, so it's got to be near him. I wouldn't say
I try to hit him, but I've got to aim in his direction, obviously.' Take that!

George Grljusich had a real baptism of fire when he when he
quit his job as an articled law clerk in Perth to join the sporting section of the Australian Broadcasting Commission in
Perth. It was only a week or two after he had settled into his
new surroundings that he found himself down at the WACA
Ground assisting in the broadcast of a game between a Combined XI and the 1960–61 West Indies touring team. George
recalls the Saturday as being a withering hot summer's day,
which was making life pretty unbearable in the ABC's broadcast box in the front corner of the old public grandstand, a
tinder-box dry wooden building which had stood for a long,
long time.

Just before the afternoon tea adjournment George was sitting in the rear of the box while his boss, Ron Halcombe, and
the doyen of cricket comments men, Johnnie Moyes, were 'up
front' describing proceedings. Ron Halcombe, a former fast
bowler for Western Australia, was a man from the 'old
school' — very upright, well-spoken and well-mannered, but
underneath it all a man with a very warm heart and a marvellous dry wit. As George sat waiting for his turn in the seat
he noticed smoke rising through one or two generous gaps
in the ancient floorboards beneath Halcombe's
seat. Obviously one of the three of them, all smokers, had
dropped a butt on the floor and it had fallen through and set
alight bits and pieces in the gap between the floor and the
wooden ceiling of the room below. Being a newcomer, George
was reluctant to interfere with the broadcast, but after a

while he realised he must do something. So, he attempted to inform Halcombe of the situation, but his boss didn't wait to hear the nature of the message and brushed him aside. George sat down in a real quandary... but when flames started licking up through the gaps he realised he had to take a firmer stand or there could be a disaster. Again he was brushed aside by Halcombe, who was lost in concentration on his work. But he persisted and eventually got the message through that, in fact, the broadcast box was on fire Panic followed. Halcombe tried to stamp it out but the source of the fire was out of reach beneath the floorboards. He then attempted to prise up some of the floorboards to get at the fire, but that also was unsuccessful. So, in a moment of inspiration, he spotted the microphone in front of him and grabbed it, shouting in his best Oxford English, 'Fire, fire... call the brigade, call the brigade... bring buckets of water, bring buckets of water...' This message went out over the air and that was the end of the broadcast, because things were starting to look grim. Fortunately, the groundsman Roy Abbott was listening to the broadcast while working in a shed out of sight of the ground. Roy gathered his men and some containers of water and dashed up to the box where they managed to douse the flames. The boys at the central fire station a couple of kilometres away must have been listening, too, because within seconds of Abbott's rescue operation they hove into sight around the corner of the pavilion, pulling hoses up the stairs to the box.

After the fire brigade had gone and everything had settled down again, there naturally arose the question of who had been responsible for the near-disaster. Halcombe could hardly blame a man of Moyes' status and he wasn't about to accept the blame himself, so the most likely candidate was the newcomer. Halcombe frowned at his new charge.

'You'll be the death of me, Grljusich,' he said.

That wasn't the end of the matter. That evening the three

were walking from the ground back to the ABC office a couple of kilometres away. Halcombe, still upset, was studiously leaving the new boy out of discussions with Moyes about the incident. Finally Moyes, feeling a bit sorry for Grljusich, said:

'I think you're being a bit hard on the youngster, Ron... how do you know it was him?'

Halcombe wasn't greatly impressed by Moyes' surmise, at which point, after having been ignored for the best part of the journey back, Grljusich decided to put an end to the matter, right or wrong.

'Well, Mr Halcombe,' he said, 'I think it was me who set the box alight by accident.'

'Why would you want to do a silly thing like that?', replied Halcombe.

George desperately tried to salvage something out of the situation.

'Well,' he said, 'perhaps it wasn't such a bad thing... I'd probably be the only Yugoslav cricket commentator in the world and how else was I going to get my name in Wisden!'

George says that Johnnie Moyes' reaction was a far cry from Ron Halcombe's!

Two people will surely remember the 1980–81 McDonald's Cup semi-final between WA and Victoria far better than anybody else. One is Darryl Smith, who at 20 years of age was making his senior interstate debut for WA. The powerfully-built all-rounder made a fairytale start in the big-time by scoring 42 scintillating runs from just 23 deliveries in the lightning-fast time of 26 minutes. The other to have the match etched in his memory is Max Walker, the Victorian fast bowler who was as experienced as Smith was green. Walker was on the receiving end of some of the roughest treatment of his career while Smith was at the crease. Smith scored three fours off Walker's seventh over, then hooked a six in the veteran Victorian's eighth. He had the crowd roaring when, in Walker's ninth over, he smacked the first two deliveries for two more huge sixes. In the end Walker claimed Smith's wicket — but only after a truly brilliant diving catch by Jeff Moss just a couple of metres inside the mid-wicket boundary. It was heady stuff and the big Perth crowd gave the young tiro a standing ovation as he left the ground after his brief but dynamic interlude.

Little did they know then that if WA was to win that match (thanks largely to Smith's big hitting) and qualify for the Cup final the following Sunday, their newfound hero wouldn't be available. The reason? He had already made plans for his marriage on the Saturday night and couldn't possibly be in Brisbane for the final the following morning.

This information came to the hand of one of the ABC radio broadcasters during the luncheon adjournment and he couldn't wait to inform his listeners. Having broken the news 'on air', the broadcaster then asked his colleague (tongue in cheek) for an opinion on a sportsman's priorities. Should a cricketer allow a simple thing like his wedding to interfere with his cricketing future?

'Oh,' said the colleague, 'I suppose we could always ask the governor to intervene and give the young fellow a stay of execution!'

There are all sorts of problems for little boys collecting autographs from sports stars. Not the least of these troubles being able to get close enough to pop the book in front of them and ask the big question. And when teams are locked in fierce combat in interstate or international cricket, players are inclined to closet themselves away from eager young whipper-snappers and their perennial autograph books. But the situation for little boys can work in reverse — too much, too soon — as was the case when the South Australian side

Englan

Keeper Bob Taylor stumps hogg in the 1978-79 series in Perth

played an up-country game at the West Australian town of Bunbury in December, 1980.

It was the first day of the school holidays and when the players arrived at the ground children, all armed with autograph books, outnumbered adults. Most of the older officials in the group who descended from the team bus wore name badges and provided no problems for the eager lads. But to a young country boy who has never been to a major city cricket venue, all players tend to look alike. The boys swarmed like an army of ants. Books were signed left, right and centre. All was going smoothly until one little fellow, about eight years old, had trouble working out just whose autograph he'd collected and whose he had not. Necessity is the mother of invention, so with a sigh, the bewildered boy walked up to the big South Australian fast bowler Wayne Prior and said in a timid voice:

'Excuse me sir, but have you seen me before?'

And talking of autograph hunters, how about this one! In the outer section of the WACA Ground during the Sheffield Shield 'grand final' between Queensland and WA at the end of the 1980–81 season an ABC broadcaster whose playing days were well behind him was recognised by one sharp lad and asked for his signature. Like bees to a honeypot every other kid in sight swarmed to beg an autograph from the ABC man. Trouble was, very few of the kids knew anything at all about the man whose autograph they were so frantically seeking. Consequently the ABC man's ego took quite a battering as he heard whispers of 'who is he?' and 'what's his name?' Still, he kept right on signing. Suddenly he looked at his watch and realised to his horror that he was due in his seat for the resumption of play in about half a minute. As he quickly finished the book he was doing, he announced to the kids remaining that he was sorry but this would have to be the last because he had to start work in a few seconds. Whatever remained of his ego was completely shattered when he heard one of the little hunters towards the rear say to his mate:

'Good ... didn't really want *his* anyhow!'

Being married to a cricket 'nut' can present its problems, as Jane Inverarity (wife of John Inverarity) has found on many occasions. The subject is never far from her husband's mind and after several years of marriage Jane found that to stay with him in conversation she had to be able to tune in to cricket at the drop of a hat. The Inverarity family left Australia during the 1975-76 season to live in England, where John was to gain teaching experience at Tonbridge School in Kent. Back home, Australia were doing battle with the West Indies.

Filled with enthusiasm for his new posting, John threw himself into school life. One lunchtime soon after they'd arrived, he burst into the house to declare to his wife with considerable fervour, 'Chapel was really great this morning!' Replied a rather bemused Jane: 'Really! Which one, Greg or Ian?'

If ever there was a devoted cricketer it is the lanky West Australian John Inverarity, whose teaching vocation took him to spend the final days of his playing career in South Australia. The move from his home State, which he had served so well for so long, was because he'd been appointed deputy principal of Pembroke School, a co-educational college in the beautiful Adelaide suburb of Kensington. When they moved, his young daughters, Alison and Kate, also attended the Pembroke junior school.

John admits he was prepared for just about anything from the co-ed experience ... but not quite for the day when he was besieged by a band of screaming banshees whom he recognised as boys from the Pembroke junior school.

'Oh please, Mr Inverarity,' they implored anxiously, 'please let Alison play in our "Test" match — she's tall and dark enough to be Joel Garner!'

It was a real batsman's game when Queensland played WA in Perth during the 1979–80 season. The home side, batting second, made a mammoth score with Greg Shipperd, Rob Langer and Ken McEwan each collecting centuries. Halfway through the third day WA had a handsome lead, but they batted on and on relentlessly. The Queensland bowlers were just about on their knees by afternoon tea but thought during the break that Tony Mann simply *must* declare the WA innings closed at that juncture. However, as the interval wore on it became obvious to the weary Queenslanders that there was to be no respite. Their captain, burly Gary Cosier, decided it was time to make a point to his opposite number. As he led his team out for yet another session in the field he stopped at the door to the WA dressingroom, poked his head in and called to Mann:

'Hey Tony, do you think we could borrow the WACA's bowling machine?'

Travelling around with a cricket team as a journalist or a radio or television commentator can be lots of fun — but it can also have its drawbacks, as one well-known (but necessarily anonymous) member of this fraternity found to his eternal embarrassment during a Test match in England. This poor unfortunate found the endless dashing from one hotel to another totally confusing and at times he became quite disorientated. One night after he'd had a good round of drinks at his hotel's piano bar, he awoke in his room on the sixth floor about one o'clock in the morning and badly needing a trip to the toilet. He groped about in the semi-darkness for the door to the bathroom, thought he'd found it and walked through. Just as the door clicked closed behind him he realised that he was, in fact, out in the passageway of the rather posh hotel. And since it was his habit to sleep 'in the raw' he was indeed in a bind. No clothes, no key to get back in and no way to even quietly call a porter to come and open his door. If he was to have one piece of luck that night it was the fact that somebody on that floor had had a meal in his room and the tray lay on the floor outside the door waiting for removal. Thankfully, underneath all the dishes and cups and saucers there was a rather soiled doily. Our suddenly-sobered hero grabbed the 'fig leaf' with many blessings and then took the only course open to him and he strode boldly to the lift. Inside he pressed the button for the ground floor, muttering a quiet prayer that the lift wouldn't stop at the first floor, where the piano bar and restaurant were situated. A cold sweat broke out as the first floor neared and when in fact the lift come to a halt there, he tried in vain to hide in a corner. The doors swung open and in walked a group of rather snooty looking people in evening dress, on their way home after a good night out. Our hero cowered in his corner, wishing he had another doily to cover his face, which he felt sure must be recognised. Down to the ground floor went the lift... And not a word was uttered during the ride. When the doors opened the other people literally ran out of the lift and across the foyer with the nude frame following them, but very carefully edging around to the reception desk. There was no spare key and finally a horrified young porter reluctantly agreed to use his house key to open the room. Back edged our hero to the lift with the porter, neither knowing which way to look. When the lift arrived it disgorged several more guests who simply couldn't believe what stood before them. But perhaps the funniest part of the whole affair was the look on the porter's face as the lift door closed behind the two of them and our hero wickedly grinned at him. The porter couldn't get down to open that room door quick enough — and neither could the journalist-cum-broadcaster, who'd had enough exposure for one night.

If there's one thing no player enjoys it's dropping catches... trouble is, they have a nasty habit of snowballing on you, too. After missing the first one, you tense up that little bit and before you know where you are, you've dropped another and so it goes on.

One club player had a terrible run in this regard and by the end of the day had put down no fewer than four catches. Admittedly two of them were really sharp chances, but still he felt really awful when he got back to the dressingroom at the close of play. Sensing that the player was really down and out, the team captain went up to him and put an arm on his bowed shoulder, saying, 'Can't be helped'. The player raised his head and shrugged:

'It isn't my day... I just know the dog's going to bite me when I get home!'

Cricket writers are, in general, an odd-ball lot. It's the little things that seem to tickle their fancy. Appreciating that fact, it's no wonder one (who shall remain nameless) can't wait for New South Wales spinner David Hourn to sire a son... just in case 'Cracker' does the right thing in the naming of the child and the heading can go up: 'Bjorn Hourn Born!'

Given his time over again, it's likely that Geoff Boycott

would choose to go into hibernation rather than make the 1978-79 tour of Australia. Boycott had a terrible time in the Antipodes. His personal problems, the loss of the Yorkshire captaincy and very ordinary (for him) batting form contributed to a nightmare tour. For once, Boycott's footwork seemed to be all wrong and this got him into all sorts of trouble, particularly on the faster wickets. He made only a few in each innings of the First Test in Brisbane and came to Perth determined to make a big score in the State game against Western Australia as a lead-up to the Second Test the following week. But he was out for just four runs in the first innings, leg before wicket. The dour Yorkshireman was far from pleased at this result, one way and another — and, true to his professional nature, was seen soon after knocking on the door of the television van at the rear of the pavilion, politely asking if he could view film of his dismissal!

One of the all-time great Australian bowlers, leg-spinner Richie Benaud, was perhaps best known among batsmen for his perfection of a delivery called the 'flipper'. It was a ball which looked for all the world like a leg-spinner, but in fact was delivered more from under the front the hand with a flipping of the fingers and came on much quicker to the batsman. Benaud practised this delivery for several years before producing it in first-class games, but when he finally unveiled it, it proved a devastating weapon in his armory. It was most treacherous when dropped short, encouraging unwary batsmen to lay back and try to pull it away through the onside. But, because it was faster and kept lower than expected, the flipper was invariably all through the batsman before he could get his bat down to cover it. The result was an embarrassing dismissal with the ball into the stumps and the batsman at sea.

Many good batsmen in Australia fell foul of the Benaud

Australian speedster Rodney Hogg — and a dropped chance

flipper until they learnt how to cope with it. Those who never got on top of it became known among the New South Wales players as 'Benaud bunnies'. West Australian all-rounder Keith Slater, who played one Test against England back in 1958–59, fell into this unfortunate category. He just hadn't a clue when Benaud sent him the flipper and time after time was bowled standing back, head up and bat raised, trying to pull the short-pitched delivery. The final humiliation came when Benaud toyed for a while, setting Slater up for the flipper, finally let one go and the skidding ball hit Slater on the toe as he lined up an almighty pull shot. The whole New South Wales side just starting laughing ... so, too, did the umpire, who raised his finger to give Slater out leg before wicket without even waiting for the appeal.

Leg-spin bowlers, like wicketkeepers, tend to be cricket's loners. They realise there's only one place in every team for a player of their type, so they give very little away, particularly to players they see as selection opponents. Malcolm Francke, a very capable leggie for Queensland in the 1960s and 1970s, was no exception. Along with a lot of other people, Francke thought he had the ability to represent Australia — but always it seemed the New South Welshman Kerry O'Keeffe pipped him for the spot in the national team.

Over several frustrating years there burned within the Queenslander a certain degree of feeling towards the man who was preventing him achieving his goal to play Test cricket. The feeling finally rose to the surface when Francke was asked his opinion on the ability of O'Keeffe. Fires lit up in Francke's eyes as he spat out:

'I would pick Kerry O'Keeffe in my *world* eleven ... to lick my boots!'

When the chirpy little Englishman Derek Randall played

club cricket in WA during the 1979–80 season he did a lot of coaching and after-dinner speaking engagements in country towns. When it came to latter, the locals sometimes didn't quite know what had hit them, what with Randall's strange accent and his unpredictable antics. One night he was involved in a question-and-answer session with some 50 farmers and workers in the dairy-farming area of Boyanup (south of Perth). The English Test star was handling the stream of cricket questions quite comfortably when out of the blue, a slightly-tipsy voice from the back of the room called out:

'Are you married, Derek?'

The sudden change of subject stopped Randall, still quite a young man, in his tracks. He thought for a while, then answered:

'As a matter of fact I am ... and for your information I've got six kids.'

From another slightly slurred voice at the rear:

'He's not a cricketer, he's a bloody rabbit!'

During the busy, busy summer of 1980–81 there were times — with Australia playing Tests against New Zealand and India plus the World Series Cup one-day competition, plus all the interstate competition — when it all seemed to be in danger of getting out of proportion. The newspapers, radio and the television were crammed with headline stories, interviews and film footage of the summer game. This blanket coverage reached a peak when the Chappell brothers figured in what will be known forever as the 'Underarm Incident' at the end of one of the World Series Cup finals against New Zealand at the Melbourne Cricket Ground. Yet, amidst the avalanche of programmes, articles and letters-to-the editor which followed that unhappy incident, at least one person reminded us that cricket, after all, is only a game. Mrs Christine Morris, of Hampton, Victoria, put it all back into perspective in a poignant letter to *The Age* newspaper. Here is the crux of Mrs Morris's message:

'One of an all-girl family, cricket to me was a noisy summer insect, until I met my husband-to-be, grandson of an Australian Test cricketer and himself a park cricketer of boundless enthusiasm and no mean ability. Suddenly I was catapulted into a whole new world, confusing to a novice but as time would prove, infinitely rewarding. Oh, those memories. The team's only "box" being hammered back into shape on the bonnet of a car, before being handed on to the next hapless victim. The glory of an infinitesimal line in the local paper, recording my husband's bowling figures. The companionship of the team barbecues, and the embarrassment of explaining to irate parents how the under-16s managed to get to the beer keg, with spectacular results. The horror of being handed what could have been a seismological chart for all I knew with the comment "you'll have to do the

The Australians in England, 1882

scoring today". The house full of a conglomeration of bats, pads and gloves, and the all-pervading smell of linseed oil and liniment. The easy wins, the devastating losses, the cliff-hanger finishes. The curtailed social life, because "it's practice tonight". Ten years later, memories are all that's left. We trek to the MCG, fortunate to be able to watch the cream of the world's cricketers, but still missing the personal involvement of belonging to a team.'

Thanks Mrs Morris!